All About the Insect World

All About
the Insect World

By Ferdinand C. Lane

Illustrated by Matthew Kalmenoff

RANDOM HOUSE
NEW YORK

SIXTH PRINTING

COPYRIGHT 1954 BY FERDINAND C. LANE

MANUFACTURED IN THE U.S.A.

Library of Congress Catalog Card Number: 54-7000

*To Emma, my wife, in appreciation of her
unfailing helpfulness and encouragement*

Contents

All About the Insect World

The Insect Wonderland

We may think we are too old for fairy stories. But science opens windows upon scenes stranger than any tales of elves or witches. And none of these is more fascinating than the wonderland of the insects. There we see strange creatures that look like tiny monsters all scales and spikes and horns. Some look more like queer machines than living things. Others are as lovely as blossoms. One and all they live out their brief lives. Some are active for a few months or days; others live only a few hours. Then they are torn to pieces or they freeze or starve to make room for other billions like themselves.

Most insects are harmless. Many are useful to us, and without them much of our vegetation would be impossible. A few are true friends and helpers.

But other species are destructive and some even threaten our welfare and our very lives. To us they seem so brutal and unfeeling that it has been said they must have been designed for some other planet.

Against such swarming enemies we are continually at war. There are even gloomy scientists who claim that such harmful insects are winning this war and may yet conquer the world in which we live. In any case, the war goes on and grows more costly all the time. And so we can see how important it is that we should know more about these curious creatures all about us that crawl and hop and fly, that serve us in so many ways but also bite and sting and injure and destroy.

What Is an Insect?

The easiest way to tell an insect from other similar creatures is to count its legs which are always six in number. Spiders and wood ticks, often called insects, have eight legs. Actually they are not insects but only distant cousins.

Anyway, there are far too many insects to include outsiders among them. A sort of census taken in 1948 showed that 686,000 species had already been described while six or seven thousand new ones were being added every year. When all the species have been listed, if they ever are, their number will probably mount into the millions, and some scientists think may even reach ten million!

Although insects differ much in size and shape, they are all alike in some ways. The body is divided into three sections: the head, the thorax or chest, and the abdomen. You can see these sections clearly in a wasp.

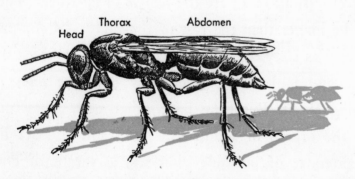

Head   Thorax   Abdomen

As in all insects, the body of the wasp is in three sections.

What a tiny neck he has, and what a slender waist divides thorax from abdomen!

The three sections of an insect's body are also divided into smaller sections called segments. The thorax has three segments, and each one bears a pair of legs. In most insects the third segment also carries wings, sometimes one pair, more often two pairs. The abdomen is usually divided into ten segments, and the legs, including the feet, nine more.

The insect's head is also divided into sections. Of these the mouth parts are most interesting. In species like the locusts, the jaws are strong. In others they are so weak that the poor insect cannot even feed itself. In some, like the mosquito, they are lengthened into a sort of tube which looks like the beak of a heron or a hummingbird.

Most curious of all are the feelers or antennae. These may be longer than the rest of the body and comprise as many as sixty segments. Or they may be short and stalky and look like horns. They help the insect in groping about. But they have other uses. They may bear the organs of sound and smell and also act like the antennae of our television sets as means of communication.

The feelers or antennae of the moth are feathery.

The head also carries the chief nerve center which takes the place of the brain in higher animals. And in some insects this nerve center has become a true brain which enables them to do many wonderful things.

Insects that live in caves may become blind, but most of them not only have three single eyes but two compound eyes as well. Those of the dragonfly sometimes have 25,000 lenses so that he can see in almost every direction at once.

The bodies of higher animals, including ourselves, are built about a bony framework with a central column or backbone. Except the teeth, all the bones are concealed within the body. The insect has no skeleton. His body is enclosed in a horny case like the armor that knights wore in the Middle Ages. This case is strengthened by a substance called chitin. It is hard and waterproof and can bend without breaking. We observe its firmness in a June bug and its toughness in a wasp or an ant.

Such body structure explains why we have so many kinds of insects. Nature can arrange bones in only a few ways. The skeleton of a man does not differ as much as we might suppose from that of a horse. But the horny case which encloses an insect's body can take on almost countless forms.

And this also allows Nature to arrange the insect's body organs in different ways. In higher animals the ears are on the head. But some gnats carry theirs on the feelers or antennae. Locusts have theirs on the first segment of the abdomen and crickets on the shins of their forelegs.

In higher animals the organ of smell is in the nose. But insects have no noses. In the cockchafer the organs of smell are on the antennae. And he may have 40,000 such organs!

Insects have a heart and a kind of circulation. But

they have no veins or arteries. Some water bugs have sacks in the knee joints which aid the heart. And insect blood is not red. Usually it is colorless, but it may be slightly green or even yellow.

In short, we might describe the insects in two words, many and varied. For not only are they far more numerous than any other visible form of animal life, but they also differ greatly in size and shape and habits.

An Insect's Curious Life Cycle

You have heard how an ugly caterpillar can turn into a lovely butterfly. But this is only one of the changes through which most insects pass in what is called their life cycle.

Usually this cycle has four stages. First come the eggs. These may be of many colors ranging through black, gray, orange, yellow, green and violet. They are of many shapes also, some with strange and beautiful markings. The housefly likes to lay her eggs in decaying matter. The locust shoves hers in masses into the ground. The mosquito arranges hers in tiny rafts upon the water. The boll weevil places hers in buds of the

Usually an insect goes through four stages in its life cycle.

Cocoon

Monarch
butterfly

These two pages show the life cycle of a monarch butterfly.

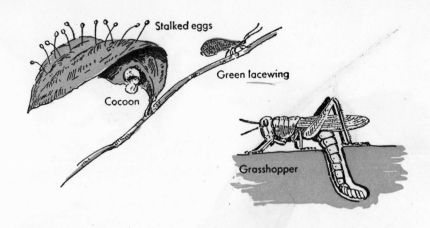

Stalked eggs

Green lacewing

Cocoon

Grasshopper

The eggs of the green lacewing seem to grow on tiny stalks.
The grasshopper shoves her eggs into the ground.

cotton plant. Many insects thrust their eggs through the tender bark of shrubs and trees. Others, like the potato bug, fasten theirs to the leaves of plants. Some do even stranger things.

With the hatching of the egg, the insect begins the second stage of its life cycle. Usually it is a wormlike creature called a *larva*. It is always hungry, for it is active and growing. This stage may last for only a few days, or it may continue for months or even years. Many larvae live underground, many in the water, others in dead wood. Those that live in the water sometimes breathe through long tubes as a diver breathes through an air hose.

Then comes the third stage, the resting period. Some larvae spin from their saliva a silken tent or cocoon to

Male giant water bug

Eggs

Egg

Boll weevil

The female giant water bug lays her eggs on the back of the male. The boll weevil puts hers in the cotton boll.

keep them warm in cold weather. Others develop a kind of shell. For the larva now becomes a *pupa*. It acts as the ground hog does when he sleeps through the winter. The great difference is that the insect's organs are changing while it rests until it has a new and quite different body.

Then comes the fourth stage, when it breaks out of the shell or silken tent or cocoon as a full-grown insect or *imago*.

This life cycle is called *metamorphosis* from Greek words which mean "a change of form." Sometimes the changes from larva to pupa to imago are so great that only a scientist can be sure he is looking at the same insect. And habits also change as much as form.

The larva crawls, the pupa stays put, the imago usually flies. The larva feeds upon the juice of plants, on leaves and many other things. The pupa does not feed at all. The imago may sip nectar from the flowers, or eat leaves or wood, or drink blood like the mosquito. In many cases it never eats.

The time spent in each stage varies greatly. Some species of wasps complete the life cycle from egg to imago in seven days. The housefly usually takes two weeks, sometimes only ten days. Some cicadas spend seventeen years underground before they come to the surface as full-grown insects. Then they live only four or five weeks. The May fly passes two or three years as larva and pupa but survives only a few hours in the open air. On the other hand, the queen of a termite colony may live fifty years.

Egg, larva, pupa and imago are the four steps in the insect's life cycle. Scientists call this *complete metamorphosis*. But metamorphosis is often incomplete. The dragonfly omits the pupa stage entirely. Some newly-hatched insects differ so little from full-grown specimens that they are not called larvae but *nymphs*. Cockroaches belong to this class.

On the other hand, some insects show more than the usual number of changes. An aphid or plant louse that lives in maple trees may develop as many as seventeen different types.

Insects in the larval or nymph stages shed their skins much as a snake does. Their body covering of chitin will not stretch and so they must break out of it in order to grow. This is called *molting*. Some species of May flies molt as many as twenty-three times.

And so the number of insect species seems all the greater because of the different forms they take in their strange life cycles.

Why Insects Are Always Small

In olden days people knew little about distant places. And so the Roman scientist Pliny wrote of ants in India that were as large as wolves and grasshoppers whose legs were so long they were used for saws! We can be glad that he was wrong. For what a world this would be if wasps were as big as eagles or cockroaches as large as lions!

But while the body structure of an insect lets Nature experiment with many forms, it sets narrow limits to their size. The outer shell serves well enough for small creatures, but it would not support such monstrous ones as Pliny wrote about. And there is another reason why insects are always small. Like larger animals they must breathe oxygen, and they have no lungs.

When you are running, your lungs start pumping in the extra air you need. But the insect cannot do this. It absorbs air much as a sponge soaks up water. Air enters its body through tiny openings called *spiracles* into tubes called *tracheae*. But air moves slowly through such openings and does not travel far, usually about a quarter of an inch. And so, few insects have bodies more than half an inch thick. Yet insects differ quite as much in size as higher animals do.

The largest are big walking sticks and beetles and moths that we shall read about presently.

The smallest are tiny gnats and midges and ants that look almost like specks of dust. Fairy flies, though per-

Air enters the insect's body by tiny openings called spiracles.

fectly formed, measure scarcely a hundredth of an inch in length. And there is a beetle which can crawl through the eye of a fine needle.

But small as they are, insects do wonderful things. True, their sight is poor in spite of their many eyes, for they can see only objects rather close at hand. But some can hear sounds we cannot hear, and others have so keen a sense of smell that they can detect odors more than a mile away.

Many insects have remarkable strength. Watch an ant moving something much larger than itself. If you were as strong, for your size, you could push a boulder weighing several tons. A good horse can drag his own weight upon the ground, but a stag beetle can drag 120 times its weight.

You can run much faster than a cockroach. But if you could run as fast in proportion to your size you could overtake a racing automobile.

A flea can jump two feet or more. If you could do as well, you could hop over an office building or leap across a river.

A tiny botfly can reach a speed of fifty miles an hour. At that rate a bird could catch a jet plane.

An insect's nerves and muscles act more quickly than

ours. A man has between 400 and 500 muscles. Some insects have 4,000. Try to catch a fly with your hand. It has only a fraction of a second to escape, but it usually does.

And now let us get better acquainted with these tiny, queer but capable creatures. We visit the circus or the zoo to see strange animals. But insects are just as interesting and much stranger. We cannot hope to meet them all. No scientist has ever done so or ever will. There are so many of them that if the names of all known species were printed in fine type in a big book two columns to a page and 100 lines to a column, they would fill a volume of 3,300 pages. And one glance at such a volume would discourage anybody. But if we follow a few prominent species for a little way, they will lead us far into that fascinating world that lies all about us, the insect wonderland.

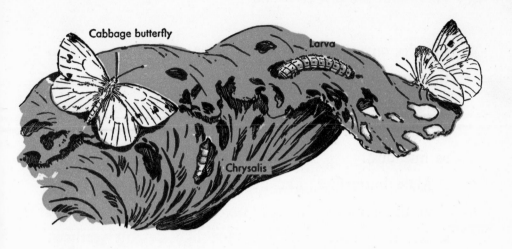

Cabbage butterfly

Larva

Chrysalis

Butterflies of Many Colors

There is a lovely fairy story about an ugly duckling that was turned into a swan. But that is no more amazing than the true story of the caterpillar that Nature changes into a butterfly. First we see a crawling caterpillar, then a pupa with withered skin. At last it spreads its wings as a butterfly to add color to the buttercups and daisies.

Butterflies and their near relatives, moths, form one of the largest classes of insects with more than 100,000 species. Scientists call them Lepidoptera which means scaly or flaky-winged. The wing is quite transparent, but it is covered with brilliant flakes or scales like embroidery upon drab cloth. These scales overlap like the shingles on a roof and may number as many as 100,000 to a square inch of surface. A big butterfly from the Amazon Valley carries a million and a half of these shiny spangles. They would rub off upon your fingers as fine dust.

Male butterflies, like male birds, dress more richly than the females. In addition to countless flakes and scales, they have tiny plumules, like downy feathers. And they may also give off pleasant odors suggesting apples, honey or even violets.

Male butterflies also fight duels in the air to win some lovely female. Among the famous scrappers are the red admiral and the pearl crescent butterfly.

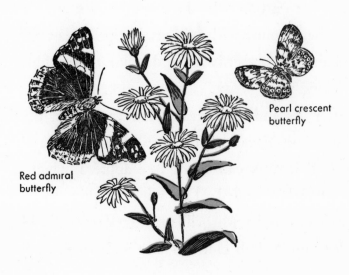

Pearl crescent butterfly

Red admiral butterfly

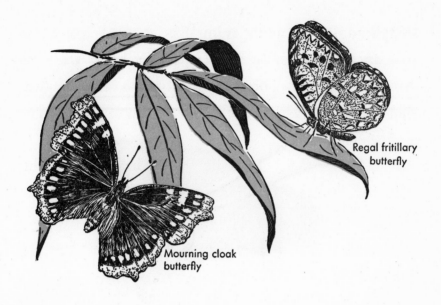

Regal fritillary
butterfly

Mourning cloak
butterfly

The bees and the ants seem always busy. But butterflies are bent on enjoying life. As caterpillars, they eat
most leaves. But each species likes certain kinds. The
painted lady butterfly enjoys thistles and sunflowers.
The sulphur butterfly prefers clover. The mourning
cloak is fond of elms and willows and poplars. The
royal fritillary hunts for violets.

Full-grown butterflies sip only liquids. Most of them
like the sweet nectar of the flowers. But others are not
so nice. The purple emperor butterflies, flying high
among the oaks, will descend, like the crows, to sample

some dead and decaying animal.

If we look carefully at a butterfly's head, we note the curious tongue. This is formed of two hollow tubes.

**The tongue of the butterfly is coiled up when not in use.
Its antennae are slender and tipped with knobs.**

When not in use, it is coiled up underneath like a watch spring. The antennae are smooth and often end in tiny knobs. The butterfly has no single eyes. But its compound eyes have many facets. Those of the swallowtail butterfly may number as many as 17,000.

Most butterflies live but a few days. The female lays her eggs of many shapes and colors, and shortly afterward she dies. But some live much longer and defend themselves in curious ways. Some give off a disagreeable odor to discourage hungry birds. The Indian leaf butterfly closes its wings and seems to disappear. This is because the central stem and the cross veins of its wings are as clearly marked upon them as the real leaves they hide among.

The mourning cloak crawls into some crevice of the bark of a tree and on a sunny day in February comes out as the ground hog does for a peep at the weather.

Fragile as they seem many butterflies travel long distances. One was observed 700 miles beyond the Arctic Circle.

The greatest wanderer is the monarch butterfly, an insect tourist which often winters in Mexico, then returns to more northern regions in the spring. As a caterpillar the monarch is anything but attractive. His fat

Monarch butterflies often travel in great swarms.

body is ringed with blue and yellow. At each end he carries two horns which he can whip about. He dines upon the leaves of the milkweed plant, then makes a pale green case or cocoon which hangs from a twig like a Japanese lantern. Inside this case he becomes a pupa. When the monarchs emerge, they collect in great swarms. In 1921 a swarm of monarchs 250 miles wide swept over Texas. It was estimated that 1,250,000 butterflies passed a given point every minute of daylight. And the flight continued for eighteen days.

Tropical butterflies are often larger and more beautiful than our own. Largest of all is perhaps the giant swallowtail from Africa with a wingspread of twelve inches. One lazy afternoon in South America I watched a swarm of brilliant blue butterflies drift past for half an hour. In the bright sun they shone like a luminous river.

And once upon a coral beach in Borneo, where pirate craft used to hide to attack great clipper ships bound for China, a big butterfly flew past with wings like black velvet. Although I was looking for strange sea shells, I chased him far up a path into the jungle only to have him get away.

Promethea moth

Eight-spotted
forester moth

Moths in More Sober Dress

Butterflies love sunlight and the bright colors of flowers. Moths prefer the shadows and the dark. And they dress in more sober hues. Many are almost white, while tints of ivory, tan and gray are common. Large moths may display pretty patterns in browns and reds and yellows. And a few are green.

Both moths and butterflies belong to the Lepidoptera or scaly-winged. But it is easy to tell them apart. We look for butterflies in the daytime and for moths in the twilight or at night. When butterflies are at rest, they hold their wings upright, often back to back. But moths let theirs droop like a fallen tent. Moths usually have plumper, wedge-shaped bodies. But a scientist would look first at the antennae. Those of butterflies are slender and tipped with knobs. Those of moths are feathery and may look like tiny palm leaves or even ostrich plumes.

Some moths grow larger than any of the butterflies. I have a specimen of the largest of American moths whose outspread wings measure nearly ten inches across. But the giant tailed moth of Madagascar has prongs upon its wings nearly six inches long. And a moth is reported in Australia with a wingspread of fourteen inches. Once, while anchored in a small port in Sumatra, I thought I saw a strange bird fluttering about the deck. But it was only a giant moth from the jungle, attracted by our lights.

The larvae of both moths and butterflies are called caterpillars. Those of the moths are particularly ugly. Perhaps the most savage looking is the hickory horned

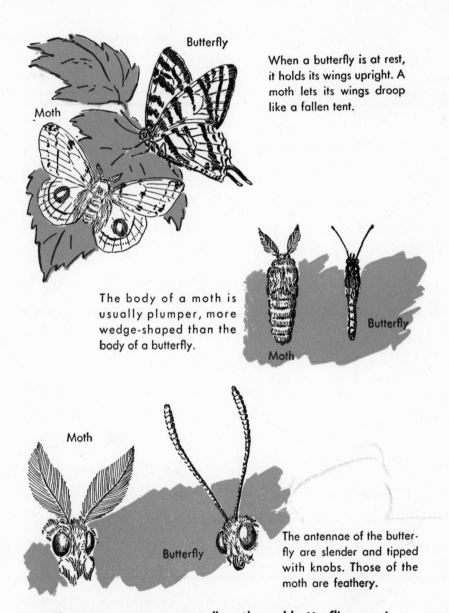

Butterfly

Moth

When a butterfly is at rest, it holds its wings upright. A moth lets its wings droop like a fallen tent.

The body of a moth is usually plumper, more wedge-shaped than the body of a butterfly.

Moth

Butterfly

Moth

Butterfly

The antennae of the butterfly are slender and tipped with knobs. Those of the moth are feathery.

There are many ways to tell moths and butterflies apart.

devil. He feeds upon the leaves of sycamores and nut trees. One would never guess that he would some day become the regal moth.

One of the loveliest of native species is the luna moth. Her wings, curved like the crescent moon, may be five inches across. Pale green they are, adorned with spots like eyes rimmed with yellow, blue and black. And her antennae are the color of yellow straw.

She never eats, and her life is short. She arranges her green-gray eggs in curving rows upon some twig. In about a week these hatch into tiny caterpillars. As they grow, their bright green suits are marked with ruby dots. Then from their mouths they send out a tiny stream of saliva which hardens into a silken thread that may be several hundred yards long. Each worker bends a leaf above it as a roof to its snug tent, which is completed in about twenty-four hours. Inside, the caterpillar curls up to become a pupa and sleeps through the long winter. Then some spring day, the full-grown moth forces its way out, lets the sun dry its drooping wings, and flies away for its brief life of freedom.

Even more splendid is the yellow emperor moth. His fat body and his wings glow as though he were dressed in cloth of gold.

The pale green wings of the luna moth may be five inches across.

Our larger moths, the Io and Cecropia and Polyphemus, have beautiful markings upon their wings. But where butterflies glitter, these have deep rich hues.

One interesting caterpillar is called the woolly bear. His body, black at both ends with a brown band in the middle, seems covered with plush. When this shaggy coat is heavy, some people claim it foretells a severe winter. But the woolly bears would smile at this if they understood. For they combine these fuzzy hairs with

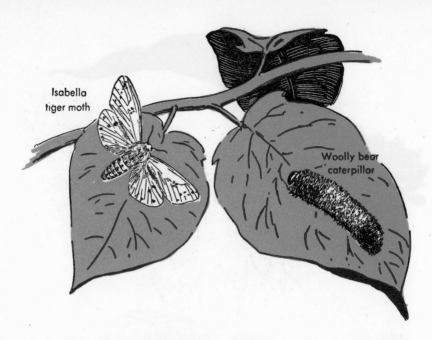

Isabella tiger moth

Woolly bear caterpillar

silky threads to make warm coverings for the winter.
And in the spring they fly away as Isabella tiger moths.

Another queer creature is the death's-head moth.
Upon its back is the outline of a human skull. When
Kaiser Wilhelm ruled Germany, one of his cavalry regiments wore a likeness of these moths upon their caps.

Death's-head moth

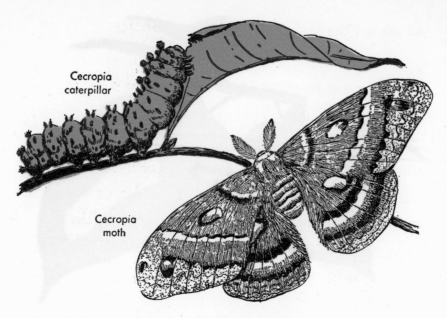

Cecropia
caterpillar

Cecropia
moth

They called themselves the Death's-Head Hussars.

Many moths never eat. But some, like the butterflies, love nectar. The hawk moth, also called the hummingbird moth, has a hollow, snoutlike feeding organ five inches long. It hovers above a flower like a hummingbird and sips nectar through this long tube or proboscis.

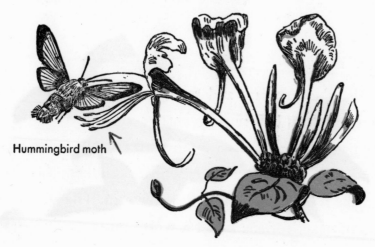

Hummingbird moth

All About the Insect World

Full-grown moths do little damage, but some of their larvae are very destructive. One of the worst offenders is the clothes moth. She does not eat, but her children are always hungry. They devour woolens and furs and feathers. They dislike the smell of cedar or camphor, and they will not eat when the temperature falls below forty degrees. Larvae of the clothes moth die when exposed to strong sunlight. So to protect our clothes we expose them to sunlight and store them in cedar chests and mothballs.

Other moths do even more damage to our gardens and our grain crops and our trees. But we'll consider them a little later when we look at insect wasters and and spoilers.

Bombyx, the Silk Maker

Many caterpillars and some other insect larvae spin silken shelters before they change into pupae. Of these the most interesting is a moth with creamy white wings some two inches across. Scientists call her "bombyx" but she is better known as the silkworm. This, of course, is a mistake, for she is not a worm but a moth in larval

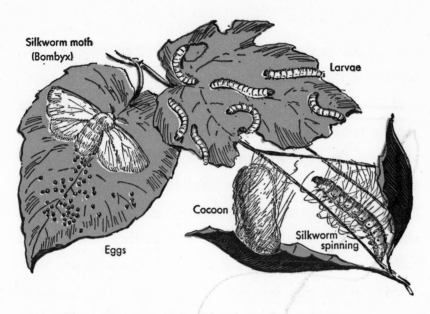

Silkworm moth
(Bombyx)

Larvae

Cocoon

Silkworm
spinning

Eggs

The moth of the silkworm has creamy white wings.

form. Many moths are larger and more beautiful. But none is so useful. She eats nothing during the few days of her brief life, but lays from 300 to 400 eggs. And it is the caterpillars, miscalled silkworms, which hatch from those eggs that are so important. In fact, while man has tamed many animals, even elephants, he has domesticated only two of the countless species of insects—the honeybee and bombyx, the silk maker.

Bombyx is a native of China where it has been held in high esteem for centuries. Because it feeds upon the leaves of the mulberry tree, millions of these trees have been planted. We should not be surprised, for bombyx must chew up nearly a ton of leaves to produce one pound of silk.

This silk is really its saliva which hardens as soon as the air strikes it. It comes from the mouth of the silkworm at the rate of about six inches a minute and may form a single thread a thousand feet long. Around and around its body this silken thread is wound to form a snug shelter called a cocoon. Inside, the weary caterpillar then falls asleep as it changes into a pupa.

Meanwhile the cocoons are gathered, and most of them steeped in hot water to kill the insects inside. The long thread is then unwound by hand. As many as 25,000 cocoons may be required for one pound of silk. A few cocoons are left undisturbed. From these bombyx gnaws her way out so that she can lay more eggs to grow more caterpillars and produce more cocoons.

In the Middle Ages silk was the chief export from China to Europe. It was carried in bales by camels across thousands of miles of desert and mountain range. Such rough and dangerous roads were known as silk routes and they were the main link between the East and West. They, too, were the work of bombyx, who was busy all the time chewing mulberry leaves and spinning cocoons. She did not know it, but she was really changing the course of history.

For a long time the making of silk was a Chinese secret. But later bombyx was brought to Mediterranean countries, and mulberry trees were planted to feed her. A small silk industry even caught on in England where bombyx has spun the silk for the robes of royalty.

Another useful worker is a lowly aphid or plant louse in India known as the laccifer. It produces the sticky substance called lac which is used in lacquer and shellac. The laccifer will eat the leaves of several different trees but prefers a kind of fig. The female insect pierces the tender bark and plasters her body with the gummy resin which oozes out. This forms a waterproof blanket to protect her from sun and rain. Beneath it she lays her eggs and dies. Her shriveled body remains mixed

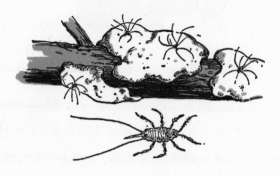

The laccifer pierces the bark and plasters her body with resin.

with the resin which is sold as lac. Some of the best variety has been made into phonograph records. If you enjoy such music remember the tiny toiler in far-off India. For a single pound of lac is the life work of 150,-000 insects.

Insects also give us bright colors. In tropical America the cochineal bug feeds upon sap from certain twigs. Its dried up body yields a brilliant dye.

Other insects pierce the buds of oak trees. A globe-like swelling forms, called an oak gall or apple. Hollow, it provides a home for many insects. But since it is nearly half tannin, it is valuable for tanning leather. And it also yields a fine brand of black ink. In Turkey

Oak gall fly

The oak gall is nearly half tannin which is used in tanning leather.

other insects cause a similar gall called a mad apple which gives us that brilliant dye known as turkey red. So while bombyx spins our silk, other insects provide some of its richest coloring.

Beetles—Big and Little

Most numerous of the insects are the beetles. Scientists list nearly three hundred thousand species.

They are sturdy creatures with powerful legs. They can bite, and some of them look very fierce. Their flying wings are enclosed in another pair of wings, horny and protective. So they are called Coleoptera which means "sheath-winged."

Among so many you will find all sorts of sizes, shapes and colors. Some bear hornlike spikes. One is even called the rhinoceros beetle. The European stag beetle has jaws that look like stag horns. It is a savage fighter. An American species is called the pinch bug.

Many beetles have shiny coats. They may glisten like gold or break up into different colors. Some are spotted like leopards or striped like tigers. Brown and black are common colors. Green beetles make a fine appearance and blue ones even more so. Larger beetles may be mottled. The harlequin beetle of the West Indies is so called because his body is queerly marked in red, white and black. The male has forelegs that may be six inches long. No one seems to know just why. Beetles are the easiest of insects to catch and preserve in your collection.

All About the Insect World

Some beetles do a great deal of harm. The long horned Capricorn beetle, in its larval form, lives in wood for three years. It can bore holes in the toughest oak. Another species also drills tunnels in wood. The female scatters her eggs along a tunnel and the larvae, hatching, bore side tunnels in various directions. As they

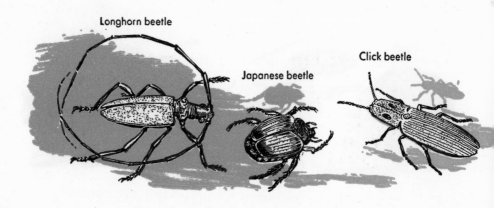

Longhorn beetle

Japanese beetle

Click beetle

seem to follow a certain pattern, they are called engraver beetles. The elm leaf beetle has destroyed many of our finest shade trees. It not only harms the trees by boring into them but lets in destructive fungi which complete the injury. Some beetles will eat but one kind of food. Others are not so fussy. Perhaps the strangest is the so-called drugstore beetle. He has been known to eat forty-five different substances including such poisons as aconite and belladonna, which did not seem to disagree with him.

A curious fellow is the bombardier beetle. When chased by a larger enemy, he escapes by emitting a drop of liquid which turns into a bluish vapor with an evil smell.

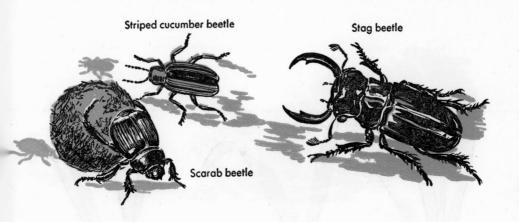

Striped cucumber beetle

Stag beetle

Scarab beetle

The blister beetle gives out an oily yellow liquid from the joints of its legs which burns like acid.

A large beetle of Mediterranean countries was held in high esteem in ancient Egypt. It was called the sacred scarab. Jewelers copied it on rings and bracelets. Even the emperor used a scarab ring to seal official documents. And scarab beetles were often buried with the dead to protect them in the next world. No other insect has been so honored. A somewhat similar American species is not so respected. We call him the tumble bug.

The sexton beetle is the undertaker of the insect world. Let it find the dead body of a creature much larger than itself, even a mouse, and it will set to work at once. It scoops out the earth beneath until the body of the mouse falls into the hole and is buried. But there is a purpose behind such activity. For the female beetle lays her eggs in the newly made grave so that her larvae, upon hatching, may be well supplied with meat.

The sexton beetle scoops out the earth under a dead animal.

The body of the Goliath beetle may be six inches long.

Beetles vary greatly in size. Some are among the smallest of insects. One of the largest is the green-winged Hercules beetle of the West Indies. His notched upper jaw may be nearly three inches long. He rather likes bananas. Still bigger is the Goliath beetle of Africa. His body may be six inches long. Place him upon a small plate, and his feet will hang over the rim. He is probably the heaviest, if not the largest, of all the insects.

The Goliath's body is beautifully marked. The wings seem covered with brown velvet. The thorax is a rich chocolate brown broken by cream-colored stripes. The antennae are blunt horns with which the male fights other beetles and also pierces the bark of vines to drink the sap. While seeking food, he gives off a sound like escaping steam. The female follows for her share of the dinner.

The larval beetle, when ready to change into a pupa, builds a mud house for itself which may be as large as a goose egg. Though relatively harmless, the Goliath is eagerly hunted by the natives of Africa. They like him made into fricassees and soups. And he is also sought after by collectors all over the world. For many years a big Goliath has kept me company in my study. I often pause before the case which holds him to admire his burly body and rich coloring.

The Water Babies

Many a small pond swarms with so much life that it seems like a little world by itself. Tiny fish swim about; turtles sun themselves on the banks; and frogs croak in the grass. But even more interesting are the insects.

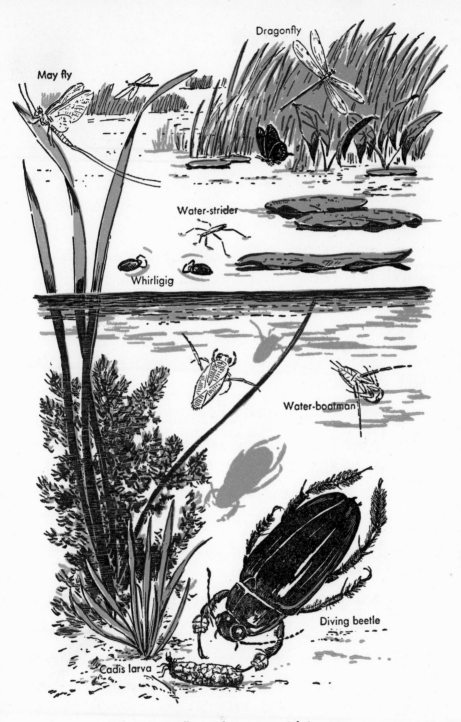

Dragonfly

May fly

Water-strider

Whirligig

Water-boatman

Diving beetle

Cadis larva

Many a small pond swarms with insects.

These are of two kinds. First are the many which develop as larvae in the water only to fly away when they are grown; and second, the true water babies which live and die upon the surface or within the depths of the water.

Among those remaining for only a short time are the mosquitoes and midges—insects hateful to animals as well as ourselves. And with them are other harmless and beautiful ones.

One of the most curious is that timid creature that we call the May fly. As a larva she may have spent three years at the bottom of some pool. Then one day she comes to the surface and crawls out among the grass. Her dry shell splits down the back. She spreads her fragile wings and flies away. How she must enjoy the sunlight! She wastes no time in eating, for her time is very short. In fact, her mouth parts are so weak she could not eat if she wished to do so. She mates and lays her eggs, perhaps in the same pool from which she has just arisen. Toward night the arc lights attract her as they do many other insects. Her one day in the fresh air has ended, and she dies. How brief are her hours of freedom after long years spent in the mud!

The caddis fly does even stranger things. When

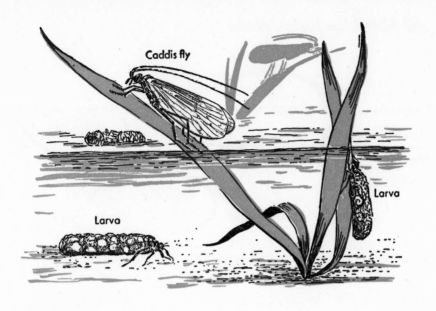

Caddis fly

Larva

Larva

grown she looks like a moth, although she belongs to quite a different order of insects. She, too, spends her larval life in the water, but we would never recognize her there. For she looks like a fat and many-legged worm. Not that she has many legs, for we know an insect has only six. But tufts of hairs along her sides give her that appearance. Unlike most insects, she builds a snug home for herself. Picking up grains of sand or bits of straw or even tiny pebbles, she glues them together in a case that may be two inches long. Inside she hides safe from the bites of hungry fish or greedy larvae. In running water she always faces her little house upstream. She even weaves a silky net in which to catch bits of food that come floating down.

These and many other insects are only larval dwell-

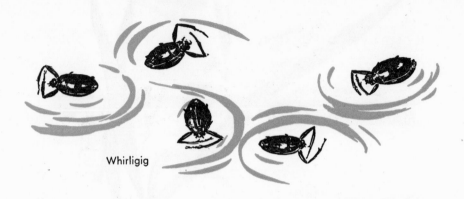

Whirligig

ers in the pools and streams. Among the permanent residents are others quite as interesting. Perhaps the most conspicuous of these are the whirligigs that go whizzing about in a way that we might think would make them dizzy. No kitten, chasing its tail, ever moves more rapidly. And unlike the kitten, the whirligig never seems to tire. As larvae, whirligigs hatch from eggs their mother fastened to the stems of water plants. They look like little centipedes and breathe through tiny gills tufted like feathers. They often feed upon the larvae of more helpless May flies. Later they crawl out along the water's edge. There they make tiny cocoons or cases for themselves in which they change to pupae and full-grown insects. Then they go whirligigging off across the water like dancers.

Many whirligigs have wings and can fly, but they seldom do so. They seem to like the water too well.

Their eyes are divided in a curious way, like those of the four-eyed fish of the tropics. With one half they gaze upward to see what is going on in the great world outside. With the other half they peer down to keep posted on affairs below the surface. Their hind legs and feet are flattened like canoe paddles. And how they can circle about! They also give off a liquid with a pleasing fragrance. Some people think it smells like apples, others vanilla. So they are called vanilla bugs. In winter they follow the good example of the frogs and turtles, diving to the bottom and hibernating in the warm mud. Then some spring day they come to the surface full of life after their long rest.

Even more curious is the back swimmer called the upside-down bug. He has a tiny boat in which he floats

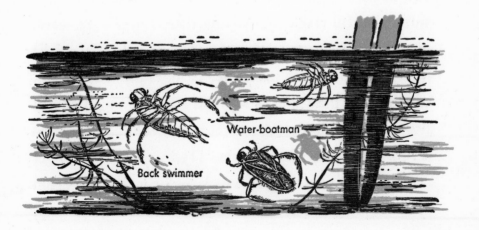

Water-boatman

Back swimmer

about. But this boat is really part of his body like the shell of a turtle. Lying comfortably upon his back, he paddles around with his broad hind feet. These are fringed with hairs that spread and contract like the webbed feet of a duck to get more power into his stroke. There he hangs, head downward, peering into the water for possible trouble or for his dinner, as the case may be.

A smaller floater called the water-boatman is often mistaken for the upside-down bug. But he is right-side-up as he paddles about. The female sometimes glues her eggs to the back of an accommodating crayfish who does not seem to object.

Such surface swimmers are harmless, but some of their larger relatives are not. For savage insects also lurk in that watery world, making life unhappy for the more peaceful residents. Among these is the water scavenger that scientists call the Hydrophilus beetle. As he feeds upon decaying plant life, he does some good, but he also likes meat and is big and strong enough to kill even young tadpoles.

Still more ferocious is the Hydiscus beetle, better known as the water tiger. As a larva he is justly dreaded by other tiny water folk. At least three inches long,

The giant water bug drains the life blood of a salamander.

he lurks in the shadows as a tiger does. He attacks not only tadpoles but small fish. And his hunger is never satisfied. As a full-grown beetle, his body, cased in armor like horn, is an inch and a half long. And he remains the same savage hunter of more peaceful life.

Still larger is the giant water bug or fish killer. When full grown, he is at least two and a half inches long. His legs, curved like those of a crab, end in needle-like hooks. He can bury these in the body of a fish four inches long and, as it struggles, drain its life blood down his greedy throat. He also kills frogs and salamanders. Not only can he swim well, but he is a fairly good flyer in spite of his size. At night he may go blundering away attracted by some distant light. So he is also called the electric-light bug. Needless to say, the fish and tadpoles he left behind hope he may never come back.

Then there are the harmless water-striders. They do not dive or even float but run about upon the surface as though skating on ice. Water-striders are slender

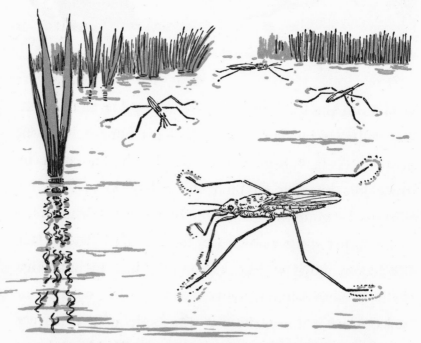

Water-striders run about on the surface of the water.

and have stiltlike legs. Their broad feet do not break through the film which marks the surface. When you fill a cup with water, you can heap it up a little if you are careful. That is what scientists call surface tension. Even a small needle may float because of this curious property of water. The water-strider never heard of surface tension, but he uses it for his own purposes. His feet make tiny impressions in the water like footprints in the snow, but they don't quite break through. Striders can fly and sometimes leave one pool for better hunting grounds. Meanwhile, they go darting about, their fore-legs half extended as though to defend themselves or snatch at food.

It may seem strange that insects shun the ocean where all life began and where so much life still remains. Fearing its great deeps and pounding waves, they prefer the quieter life of stream or pool. Of all the many species of insects that may mount into the millions only a few water-striders have put to sea. Perhaps they were bolder or more adventurous than the others. The female often fastens her eggs to the feathers of some sea bird that bears them far away. A favorite haunt of theirs is the Sargasso Sea, that mysterious region of floating seaweed stretching across the Atlantic beyond Bermuda. There the water-striders race about from one floating meadow of seaweed to another. And there many of them are born and live out their strange lives hundreds of miles from any land.

Dragons of the Air

Dragonflies are like fairy airplanes. Over marsh and pool they dart and wheel as though from sheer love of flying. But they are really hunting. Like hawks they sweep upon mosquitoes, flies and other insects that form their food. Their legs, covered with hair, fold like a basket to clutch their prey. Their bulging eyes may have as many as 25,000 lenses. So while in motion they can look up and down as well as from side to side. In bursts of speed they can go a mile a minute. One big dragonfly, when caught, was carrying more than a hundred mosquitoes in its mouth. Another ate its own weight in flies in half an hour. To such insects dragonflies must seem like true dragons of the air.

Rather large, with slender bodies and stiffly outspread wings, they have been accused of many things. In older times people called them devil's darning needles and

Dragonflies dart and wheel over marshes and pools.

claimed they could sew up the lips of wicked people. In the South they are known as snake doctors and mule killers. But these are idle tales. Dragonflies are not only harmless to man but extremely useful, for they destroy numberless harmful insects.

And dragonflies are beautiful. They add many a touch of color to the waste places which they love. Their long bodies may be dressed in green and gold. Or they may glow in red, black, brown, blue, and even royal purple. Their wings, many-veined and quite transparent, seem spun from gauze. It is no wonder they have been called living rainbows.

The dragonfly, though a savage hunter, lives a dangerous life. Fish jump for it as it skims above the water. Frogs snatch it with their long tongues. Hungry birds find it a tasty morsel. And when hunting is poor, big dragonflies will pounce upon smaller relatives.

Dragonflies can travel long distances. They have been known to cross wide arms of the sea. For like the frigate bird and the albatross, they are most at home in the air. They never walk or run like flies or ants. But they can climb and when at rest cling to some friendly twig as a bird does.

Like the mosquitoes that she hunts, the female dragonfly usually lays her eggs upon the water. Covered with a kind of jelly they sink to the bottom. But sometimes she dives beneath the surface, her body covered with a film of air. Piercing the stem of some water plant, she tucks her eggs inside. But whether there or in the mud, they hatch in two or three weeks into tiny creatures known as nymphs. These breathe through gill slits like fish. And by forcing out water through these slits they move around. As they grow, they molt. They are always eating with mouth parts that are large and ugly. The under lip is so long that it folds back between the front legs. When thrust forward it has claws to hook its prey. The nymph feeds mostly on water insects but sometimes will attack small fish.

Two or three years may pass in this way among other water babies. Meanwhile, the nymph grows larger and darker in color. Then one day it climbs a stalk of grass or water plant. Its shell splits down the back, and after a struggle it crawls out, a full-grown dragonfly. It waits for its wings to dry and harden in the sun. Then off it speeds for a new and different life of adventure in the upper air.

The Praying Mantis

A true tiger of the insect world is the praying mantis. For in savagery it has few equals in all nature. Though it belongs to the order of the crickets and the grasshoppers, these have little cause to love their ferocious relative. For every year great numbers of them fall victims to the cruel hunger of the mantis.

Yet its looks deceive not only other insects but the men who named it. These were missionaries in the Far East. When they saw a mantis standing upright and motionless, with its big forelegs raised and drooping, they thought it joined with them in prayer. But the mantis was not praying. It was waiting for some other insect to come within reach of its deadly clutch.

Its body, which may be four inches long, though slender, is powerful. Its front legs—we might call them arms—are lined with sharp spikes. Once crushed between them, even the deadly black widow spider is doomed. The mantis will also eat hairy caterpillars. Some tropical species are said to kill even toads and small birds. Perhaps the only insects that the mantis seems to dislike or avoid are certain species of ants.

The mantis has been called the one insect with a true face. If so, that face would make a mask for Halloween. Broad at the brow with bulging eyes, it narrows to the cruel jaws beneath. But it does seem to have a solemn, peaceful expression, quite unlike its savage nature.

The mantis is one of the few insects that can turn its head. One scientist said, "It is the only insect that can look over its shoulder, wash its face like a cat, eat from your hand like a dog, and drink water like a horse."

The baby mantis is little larger than a mosquito. Light yellow with dark eyes, it molts and changes color to blend with the green leaves. Though some species are fairly common in this country, they are hard to find. One will remain motionless for hours. It can move about but may stay on the same shrub or bush for days. Then in the fall, when fully grown from eating countless other insects, it mates. But it remains savage to the end. For the female mantis, larger and stronger than the male, then turns upon her unfortunate husband, crushes his head in her sharp jaws and feeds upon his body.

The last act in the cruel drama of her life then takes place. She squeezes a white froth from her abdomen. Hanging head downward, she twists about in widening circles, weaving a ball as large as a walnut. In this she lays her eggs which may number 200 or more. At first white, the froth hardens, toughens and turns brown. It protects the eggs from winter cold. This done, the savage mother then stalks off in search of insect prey. But usually her days are numbered. For when frosts come she dies.

The European mantis has been brought to America

and so have several Oriental species. They seem contented and have spread everywhere. Though we dislike their cruelty, we must admire their courage. They seem to have no fear. A big mantis will stand up to defy a bird or even a kitten.

Much as it is dreaded by other insects, the mantis is a friend to man. In the Far East one is sometimes fastened by a thread to a bedpost as a protection against other insects. No watchdog is more faithful. In captivity a

The female mantis kills the male and feeds upon its body.

mantis will readily eat chopped beef or dine upon a dead cockroach. It makes an interesting pet. One old lady even had a tiny silver collar made for her pet mantis and carried it about perched upon her shoulder where it was fastened by a little chain.

Queer Sticks That Walk

Someday while in a woodland you may notice a twig go moving off among the leaves. You may even rub your eyes and wonder if you are "seeing things." And you would be, for there are few stranger creatures than those insects that we call walking sticks.

The name is well chosen. They look so much like sticks that they deceive even the birds or field mice which might find them tasty morsels. True, like other insects, they have six legs. But these are so slender you could easily overlook them. Besides, when they are at rest, walking sticks often thrust their front legs straight before them and fold the other four close to their bodies. A favorite trick of theirs is "playing possum" or appearing to be dead. They can remain motionless for several hours. Then they look and act like sticks.

The walking stick looks like part of the plant it feeds on.

These insects are fine examples of Nature's ways of protecting her children. They look so much like the plants they feed upon that their enemies fail to see them. And many change color with the season. In springtime they are green like the young leaves. But as these turn brown and rusty in the fall, so do the walking sticks. It is a splendid example of Nature's camouflage.

In tropical countries such camouflage goes even further. For there, walking sticks often seem covered with bark. And they may have queer lumps that look like buds.

While in the woodland, you may hear a pattering upon the fallen leaves like drops of rain. As you look up to see the sun shining brightly, you wonder what is happening. This queer sound may be only the female walking sticks, and most of them are females, laying their eggs. They let them drop upon the ground to be hidden among the leaves. In places where "sticks" are numerous, you might find several dozen eggs upon every square foot of ground. And they may lie there for months when perhaps scarcely one in a hundred will hatch. In some species the eggs look like tiny black seeds with a white stripe on one side. In England, where walking sticks feed upon rose bushes, gorse and other plants, these eggs may resemble tiny jars with a lid on one end and a button in the center of the lid. When grown the little walking stick curled up inside pushes off the lid, stretches his long legs, straightens his cramped back and goes off in search of some tender leaf for breakfast.

He looks much like his mother but molts or sheds his skin several times before he is fully grown. Meanwhile, if one of his legs breaks off he can grow another, although it takes him some months to do this.

There are several species of walking sticks in America.

In the South a fairly large "stick" gives off a bad-smelling liquid that would smart badly if you got some in your eye. It does this to discourage hungry birds that may be observing it with interest. Children call it a "musk mare."

Our walking sticks can only get about on crooked legs. In tropical countries some "sticks" have wings. And there they grow much larger. In fact, the giant walking sticks of the East Indies are perhaps the largest of all insects although one or two of the beetles would dispute this. Specimens have been reported that were fifteen inches long. While I am writing, a big tropical "stick" looks down upon me from a frame upon my study wall. I asked a dealer in New York to get it for me, but ten years passed before he could fill my order. Then one of those collectors who roam far-off places searching for butterflies, orchids and other curious things sent him five of the giant walking sticks from the great island of New Guinea. And mine was the largest of the lot.

Walking sticks eat the leaves of some trees and shrubs. But they are otherwise quite harmless as they creep awkwardly about just as they have been doing for millions of years.

The True Bugs

Many people call all insects bugs. They even include ticks and spiders which are not even insects. Such a definition is much too broad.

In England, when people mention bugs, which they seldom do, they mean bedbugs only. And that definition is too narrow.

When the scientist speaks of bugs he means the order of *Hemiptera*, insects with mouth parts for sucking the liquids which form their food.

Largest of the bugs is the cicada. The female has an

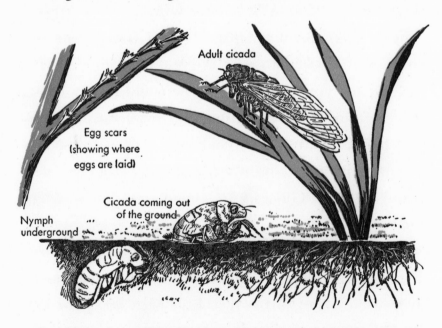

Adult cicada

Egg scars
(showing where
eggs are laid)

Cicada coming out
of the ground

Nymph
underground

One kind of cicada lies buried in the ground seventeen years.

ovipositor as sharp as a chisel. With it she cuts through the bark of a twig to deposit her eggs. The larvae, on hatching, fall to the ground and burrow beneath the surface. There they grow by sucking the juices of roots. One species lives buried in the dark for seventeen years. And so it is called the seventeen-year locust, although it isn't really a locust at all. And then at long last it appears a winged insect to pipe its shrill songs for the four or five weeks of its brief life in the sun.

Berry pickers often pick bugs with a disagreeable odor called stinkbugs. Quite harmless, they are merely trying to protect themselves with that ugly odor. Squash bugs do much the same thing, but they also damage our gardens. And the chinch bug is one of our worst enemies. For in sucking the juices from growing vegetation he destroys whole fields of hay and grain. The kissing bug has a name which does little to offset his bad habits. For he bites sleeping people on lips or face, causing sores that may spread disease.

An odd fellow is the frog hopper. He is "forever blowing bubbles." Sucking the juice from a grass stem, he pumps out some of the liquid in bubbles until he is covered with a white froth. This protects him from the sun and from savage insects. He is quite small, scarcely

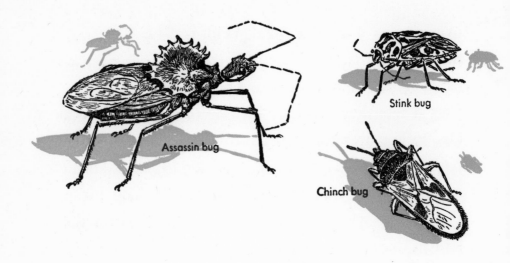

Assassin bug

Stink bug

Chinch bug

a quarter of an inch long, and is greenish yellow in color. Cool and comfortable in his odd house, he develops wings and flies away.

Some bugs serve us by killing harmful insects. Among these is the assassin bug. At least potato beetles would call him so, for he kills numbers of those striped pests of the potato field.

Another terror to insects is the ambush bug. Green and brown with black markings, he hides among the flowers. His eyes are yellow, and he keeps them peeled for some unfortunate bee or butterfly which may approach too near. Though he is scarcely half an inch long, he has cruel claws and a poison beak which folds up neatly beneath his head. With this he can easily kill other insects and suck the juices from their bodies. When the flowers fade on his particular bush, he flies off to another to wait for new victims.

Most numerous of the bugs are the aphids or plant lice which do so much injury to trees and plants. They breed in a curious way. Through the summer one generation follows another, all females. Later another generation appears with wings. Borne by the winds, they sail away sometimes for miles. In autumn males are also born. These mate with females which lay eggs that hatch in the spring to start a new generation of females in their strange life cycle.

Many insects prey upon the aphids. Noteworthy is the larva of the lacewing fly. Sometimes called the aphis lion, this creature can destroy aphids at the rate of one a minute. The poor aphid can defend itself only by smearing a gummy wax on the face of its attacker.

But we need not pity the aphids. They swarm in such numbers that we can scarcely imagine what might happen if they did not have so many enemies. Dr. Lee Strong of the U. S. Bureau of Entomology tells us that if a single pair and their offspring could reproduce undisturbed for one year, they would create enough aphids to fill the entire Atlantic Ocean.

Our Friends the Bees

Most insects live lonely lives. They fight their own battles and survive by their own efforts. Even when they gather in swarms like locusts they are much like a crowd at a ball game. But there are insects which have developed societies in which each member works for the common good. They are called "social insects," and we can never cease to wonder at their strange customs.

Among higher animals the male is usually larger than the female. But in the world of the social insects all life centers in the queen. And almost all the insects which she rules are females.

Ants and termites are social insects. And so are some of the many species of wasps and bees.

Of special interest are the bees. They are the most useful of all insects. And when we speak of bees we mean honeybees. There were perhaps five thousand species of wild bees in North America when honeybees were brought over from Europe. But the honeybees are more important than all the others.

There are three classes among them: the queen, the few males, and the undeveloped females or workers that may number many thousands.

The queen is larger than the others. She has a sting which she never uses except to fight rival queens. She does no work except lay eggs and is fed and tended by the workers.

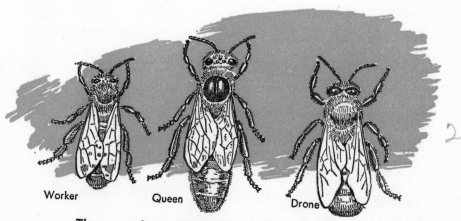

Worker Queen Drone

There are three different classes of honeybees.

All About the Insect World

Aside from one important function which we shall note later, the males do little except eat and make a nuisance of themselves. They are called drones, and that is where we get our name for an idle fellow. They are larger than the workers, have no stings, and can scarcely feed themselves. Their bodies are covered with soft brown down.

Of greater interest is the worker. And she *is* a worker. Where we have two eyes, she has five. On each side of her head is a compound eye with more than six thousand facets or lenses. Between them in a little triangle are three single eyes. Her long tongue, when not in use, is folded under her head where her chin ought to be. It is protected by horny sheaths. She has neither ears nor nose, but her two antennae carry thousands of tiny spots that act as organs of smell and hearing. The antennae are covered with fine hairs to help her grope about in the dark hive. They also serve her as a voice. For when two workers meet, they cross antennae as we clasp the hand of a friend. And at times they seem to converse in a bee language of their own.

The worker has two pairs of wings. At rest, the smaller pair is folded under the larger. But in flight, little hooks on the underwing fit into grooves on the

Wing

Thorax

Antenna

Abdomen

Pollen basket

Antenna cleaner

Wax scales

Stinger

Pollen combs

Spurs for prying off wax

The body of the worker bee is a marvel of complicated equipment. On her legs is a complete set of the tools she needs.

upper. If they were not fastened, the worker could not fly well.

Still more wonderful are her legs. Upon them is a complete set of the many tools she needs. These include combs, brushes, scrapers and nippers. Each of her six feet is tipped with a sticky pad for smooth surfaces and a claw for clinging to rough places. On her hind legs are also tiny baskets formed of stout hairs for storing the pollen which she gathers from the flowers.

Upon her abdomen she carries a weapon of defense, her sting. This is formed of two slender shafts, each notched with ten barbs. As she drives them in, she injects formic acid mixed with other poisons. One sting can raise a painful swelling and several may cause death. But she can use her sting only once. For when the barbed shafts are torn from her body, she dies.

Bee Life in the Hive

We may think of a beehive as a tiny house. But it is more like a city. For it may shelter many thousands of bees.

As soon as the worker is full grown, she begins tidying up the hive. Then she is sent out to collect a brown substance called propolis or bee glue. She scrapes this mainly from the buds of poplar and cherry trees and brings it back in her pollen baskets. With it she covers

Newborn bee

Queen

Workers

Queen cell

Workers with pollen

Guards

Worker delivering nectar

Inside the beehive worker bees slave for their queen.

rough places inside the hive just as we plaster walls or ceilings. She also fastens honeycombs in place.

After a few days she has learned to use her wings so that she can take longer trips for nectar. This is the sweet liquid (it may be over one-third sugar) that many blossoms make to attract insects like herself. She swallows the nectar into a little sac inside her body called the honey sac, where it is changed into honey. From some blossoms she also scrapes off that yellow dust called pollen which she stuffs into her pollen baskets. These may hold 100,000 pollen grains.

Usually she does not venture out more than half a mile. But she may range four or five miles. She can fly from five to eight miles an hour. Eighty thousand field trips may yield only enough nectar for one pound of honey. Such trips, added together, would take a bee twice around the globe. What a distance to go for a pound of honey!

In the hive the worker empties the contents of her honey sac into a cell of honeycomb where it is allowed to "ripen" for several days. In other cells the pollen is stored. Mixed with nectar and a little honey, it becomes yellowish brown "beebread." We would think it bitter, but the bees like it.

Honey and pollen would be of little use if there were no place to store them. And in making storage bins the bees are among the most expert builders in the world.

The wax for their wonderful combs, or storage bins, is derived from honey. Bees must eat from three to twenty pounds of honey to manufacture one pound of wax! This wax seeps out beneath the workers' abdomens into tiny cups placed there by Nature. Chewed and mixed with saliva, the wax can be spread in thin bands. The bees shape these bands into the cells of the honeycomb which always have six sides. Scientists tell us that

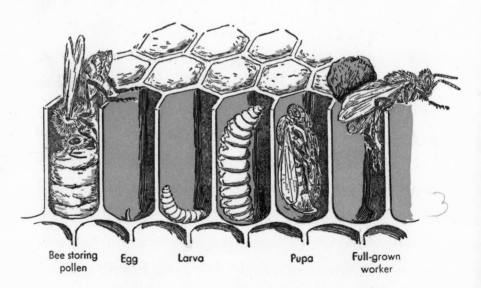

Bee storing pollen   Egg   Larva   Pupa   Full-grown worker

Cells of the honeycomb always have six sides.

such a cell provides the most space from the least material. Some cells are storage bins for honey and beebread. Others are cradles for bee babies.

The queen bee lays a single egg in each cradle cell. In most of them she places fertile eggs which will hatch thousands of workers and a few queens. But in others she lays infertile eggs that will develop into drones.

In about three days the eggs hatch into tiny grubs or larvae. At first they are fed with royal jelly, a milky liquid which oozes from glands in the workers' heads. Later honey and beebread are added to the menu. In a few days the larval worker has grown until she nearly fills her cradle cell. Feeding then ceases and a porous wax cap is placed over her head. She now enters the pupal stage of an insect's curious life cycle. A few days later she gnaws her way out as a full-grown worker. About three weeks have passed since the egg was laid.

The egg which produces a queen is exactly like that which produces a worker. But it has been laid in a larger cell. And the tiny grub is stuffed with royal jelly until in sixteen days it becomes a full-fledged queen.

And she *is* a queen! Her one duty is to lay eggs. She can lay as many as 3,000 in a day or perhaps 100,000 in a season.

The workers are always active. And that is why we say "busy as a bee." Not only do they keep the hive clean, go on long field trips for nectar and pollen, and manufacture the honeycomb, but they do other things quite as remarkable. They even have their own way of "air-conditioning" their hives. At the entrance to the hive the workers gather to vibrate their wings. These move so rapidly—up to 400 times a second—that they become invisible. This movement creates air currents which ventilate the hive. At the cells where other workers have emptied their honey sacs, similar groups gather to evaporate the water content and "ripen" the honey. And in the brood chamber where baby bees are lying, the workers keep up an even temperature.

The workers are always cleaning themselves with the combs and brushes on their legs. They are more active than any kitten. For they have six legs instead of four, and they can move them about in any direction.

As the queen keeps on laying eggs and new bees are born, the hive becomes too crowded. Then the queen decides to seek a new home. The workers, or most of them, go with her. But first they gorge with honey as if on a grand celebration. Then some fine spring morning the queen leaves the hive, followed by a cloud of

Workers cling to the queen and to one another in a swarm.

workers. She alights perhaps upon the limb of a tree where she clings while the workers cling to her and to one another in a great mass or swarm. Then it is that the beekeeper can capture the swarm and move it into an empty hive.

Meanwhile, in the old hive a new queen emerges

from her brood cell. She goes at once to the other brood cells and stings the younger queens to death. When two queens emerge at about the same time, they fight for the empty throne until one is killed.

The new queen then takes a strange journey. She flies straight up toward the sky to escape possible enemies. The drones follow her. When the strongest or most active overtakes her, they mate in mid-air. The drone, dying, then comes tumbling down while the queen crawls back into the hive, ready to lay eggs. The other drones are allowed to stay in the hive. But as autumn approaches and food supplies fail, they are thrust out of the hive to starve. This seems cruel, but we need not feel too sorry for the drones. They have lived in idleness while the poor workers worked themselves to death. For they often die when scarcely six weeks old. A few, born in the late season, live through the winter with the queen waiting for spring to bring back the flowers with new treasures of nectar and pollen. The queen may survive four or five years.

Bees carry pollen from one apple blossom to another.

Our Debt to the Bees

One valued gift from the bees is honey. In this country we eat nearly 200 million pounds every year.

There are at least two dozen brands of honey, depending upon the blossoms which yield the nectar. White clover honey is the favorite. If a hive is near a clover field, the bees will pass all other flowers to reach the clover. We also have honey gathered from fields of buckwheat and from orange blossoms.

Beeswax is also a useful product of the hive. It helps to polish our floors and furniture. It stiffens candles so that they do not melt too quickly. It adds body to cold creams and shaving mixtures.

But bees do more than give us wax and honey. Some of the pollen they collect to make beebread sticks to their bodies. When they burrow into other flowers, it is brushed off on the new blossoms. Many plants need the pollen from other flowers in order to form their own seeds. This is called cross-pollination and forms a wonderful chapter in the great story of creation.

Our fruit trees and berries need insects to bring pollen from other blossoms. So do cotton plants and the clover and alfalfa that dairy farmers raise. So do many vegetables in our gardens. To be sure, other insects help in this good work, even some of the flies. But it is estimated that honeybees alone do half of the cross-pollination which produces two billion dollars' worth of crops in this country every year. And so scientists tell us that for every five dollars' worth of honey and wax the bees give us, their labor in developing seed crops is worth at least one hundred dollars.

Farmers and fruit growers often rent hives of bees to pollinate their fields and gardens and orchards. There are about six million bee hives in this country. At times a hundred or more are loaded, by night, on a big truck and carried long distances where they are most needed.

And so, for many fruits and vegetables as well as for wax and honey, we must thank our good friends the honeybees.

The Wasps and Their Queer Ways

There are two classes of wasps: the social species that form great communities like the bees, and all the others that live and forage for themselves. Both kinds are extremely interesting.

The social wasps were the first paper makers. Among them are the yellow jackets and the white-faced hornets. The yellow jacket is slender and quite splendid in his bright coat. The white-faced hornet is more stocky with a stouter waist. And how he can sting! A bee will light and drive in her sharp lancets. But a hornet darts like an arrow and strikes sting first. Woodsmen tell tall stories of his painful stings.

These and several other species of wasps have strong jaws. They bite chunks of wood from old fences or trees and chew them into pulp like that from a paper mill. First they hang their roof by a stout paper cord from a branch or rafter. Under this roof they attach layer after layer of six-sided cells as the bees do. But

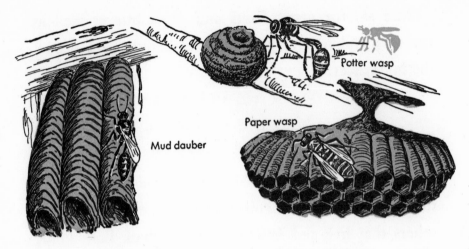

Wasps build nests of many shapes and sizes.

Mud dauber

Paper wasp

Potter wasp

wasps use paper instead of wax. They then enclose the nest in stout walls of paper, smoothing it and even measuring its thickness with the tools attached to their legs. Paper is a good protection against the weather, as the Japanese learned when they made rooms with paper walls. But the wasps had discovered that long before.

Usually wasp paper is streaked with gray. In my home I have a nest as large as a water bucket. But such nests are sometimes much larger. One built in the garret of an old English house was five feet around. It could house 50,000 wasps. In the tropics wasps build hanging nests four feet long or more. One species has nests called Dutchman's pipes which they resemble.

Their walls are almost as strong as cardboard and shed rain easily.

In northern climates the queen is usually the only wasp that survives the winter. Born late in summer, she mates with a male wasp, then crawls into some nook to wait for spring. She then sets to work building a nest. In the first cells she lays eggs which hatch into worker wasps. These add new cells and care for the larvae. When their saliva is spent in paper making, they forage for food. They love nectar and the juices of ripe fruits and berries. But they chase flies or cut caterpillars in pieces into insect hamburger to feed the larval wasps. For these are meat eaters. Late in the season the males are born and mate with new-born queens. Meanwhile, the old queen has stopped laying eggs; the workers have little to do, and a great change takes place in the nest. The laws which governed it have broken down. The young queens and males fly away; the workers fall upon the larvae and sting them to death or throw them out. Then they, too, leave the old home which is never occupied again. They range the fields or find their way into our houses where they are a nuisance. But their time is short. For with killing frosts they die.

But the social wasps are not the only builders. Among

the many other species are some quite as skillful. Noteworthy are the mud daubers or mason wasps. They too have queer houses, but these are for their children, not themselves. The female mason moistens dirt with her saliva and carries a tiny pellet to some favorable site. This is often the side of a building. Sticking the pellet there she lets it dry. How she welcomes a mud puddle where the soil is already moist! One upon another she piles her pellet bricks until the cone-shaped hut, perhaps an inch high, is finished. Then she goes hunting. Pouncing upon a fat caterpillar, she stings it, not to kill but to paralyze, and stuffs it into her little house. When this is nearly filled, she lays an egg inside and adds a mud roof. The egg hatches into a grub which feeds upon the still living caterpillars. By spring, it is a full-grown wasp. Then it forces its way out to begin a new generation.

A mason wasp will build several of these queer houses. But she never sees any of her children. For neither she nor her mate survives the winter. In India people still live in mud huts. And the adobe houses of our own Southwest are much the same. But mason wasps were expert builders long before men.

Of the 10,000 species of wasps a few hundred are

social while the others are like lone wolves. And some *are* wolves! Many, like the bumblebees, dig snug holes or burrows in the earth. Among these is the digger wasp. It will send up a stream of dirt particles like a dog after a woodchuck. When underground, it digs long burrows with branching tunnels. Like the mud daubers, it stores living food for its young, for it has no icebox to preserve it. One will drag a caterpillar much heavier than itself through the rank grass. Or, carrying some smaller insect through the air, it will drop it over the burrow entrance. A tiny digger preys upon plant lice or aphids. She will store as many as fifty of them underground. Just as the bees prefer a certain flower, wasps often prey upon a single species.

One such killer attacks only the cicada or seventeen-year locust. This is too heavy to carry far. And so she climbs some shrub or tree, dragging the cicada, then starts for home on a long slant like a glider plane. Such a flight may be repeated several times. Safe in her burrow, she lays an egg upon her helpless victim to provide her own larvae with food.

Some wasps attack only spiders. And this seems just, for spiders live almost wholly upon insects. Besides wasps may get tangled in the deadly webs of the spider.

Even the largest of the spider family, the tarantula, falls victim to a fearless wasp called the tarantula hawk.

After a desperate duel, the tarantula hawk wasp usually defeats the tarantula spider which is much larger.

The tarantula is much the larger, for his outstretched legs can cover a saucer. And his cruel jaws carry poison fangs. But the wasp is much the quicker and after a desperate duel usually defeats its dangerous foe.

The lifetime of the wasp seems brief compared with that of some other insects, but it is crowded with adventure.

Those Wonder Workers—the Ants

Bees and wasps do remarkable things, but ants show even more intelligence. Among all the insects their customs most resemble ours. For ants build cities. They lay out roads and dig tunnels. They store food in granaries. Some even plant and cultivate gardens. They keep "ant cows." Sad to say, they also wage war among themselves and make slaves of weaker ants. In short, they have a strange civilization of their own.

Ants live much longer than bees. Where the poor bee often works herself to death in six weeks, ant workers may live for seven years. The queen bee has a life span of four or five years, the queen ant perhaps eighteen. Bees eat honey and beebread. Ants will eat almost any kind of food.

Tiny as they are, ants show an amazing hold upon life. One ant lived under water nearly three days. Another went eight days entirely without air. And still another survived forty-one days with its head cut off.

There are thousands of species of ants. Some are nearly an inch long. Others look like specks of dust. And in their habits they differ quite as much as human beings.

Most ants live underground. But carpenter ants fashion homes in dead trees or even the floors and timbers of old houses. Wood ants use pine needles as boards and rafters to make dwellings several feet high and many feet across.

When ants swarm, males and females fly off together in a great cloud, for both have wings. Then they scatter. Most of them die, but wherever a male and female ant alight, they begin digging a home in the ground. The male does not live long, but the female faces months of toil. Because her wings are a nuisance, she breaks or even bites them off. In the underground chamber she begins laying eggs which hatch into legless larvae or grubs. Since she has no other food, she feeds them with her own saliva. When very hungry she will eat a few of her own eggs. But she has been known to go entirely without food for nearly a year.

The grubs spin tiny coverings to form cocoons. Inside they become pupae and finally gnaw their way out. New-born ants, like most bees, are workers. They help the mother ant dig larger rooms and forage for food. Several years may pass before the colony is well established. And then the mother ant forsakes toil for leisure. She is now a true queen. She does nothing but lay eggs and enjoy her meals. Among tropical ants she may grow

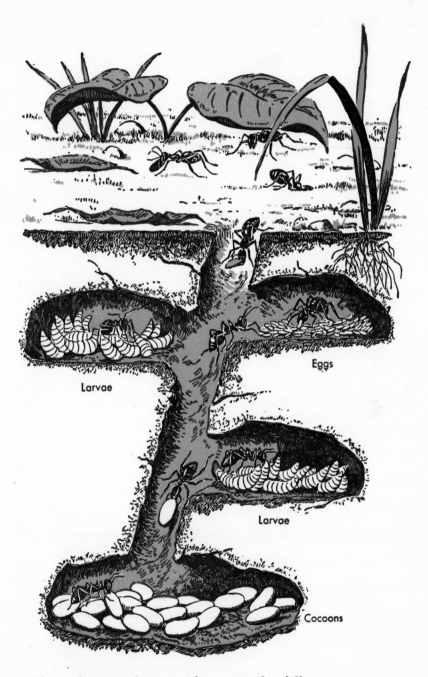

Larvae

Eggs

Larvae

Cocoons

The underground ant nest has rooms for different purposes.

until she is a hundred times larger than her workers. But unlike the jealous queen bee which stings her sisters to death, the ant queen welcomes younger queens to increase the colony.

Bees have a honey sac to hold nectar. Ants have a similar sac called a "social stomach," for an ant often shares the contents of its stomach with other ants.

The bees have but three classes—queens, males and workers. The ants usually add a fourth class—the soldiers. They guard the home or go on raiding parties. Larger than the workers, they have big heads and jaws. Some have stings like the bees. Most species bite. Their saliva is mixed with the formic acid which makes a bee sting so painful. In fact, this acid was named for the ant which ancient Romans called a formica.

Bee workers do many tasks. But ants develop distinct classes. More than twenty types of workers have been described. Strangest of all are those which become living storage tanks of honeydew, the sap of certain trees and plants. They are gorged with this sweet liquid until their social stomachs swell like tiny balloons. Year after year they hang to the roof of the nest. Workers stuff them with honeydew which they sample later. Perhaps nowhere else can we find such self-sacrifice.

The bees make wax cradles for baby bees. Ants often carry cocoons containing unborn ants about with them. These cocoons are miscalled ant eggs, but they are ant pupae, not real eggs.

In the nest a worker will clean its own body, as a kitten does, perhaps twenty times a day. Sometimes it will curl up like a dog and go to sleep. When it wakes, it stretches and even opens its jaws as though yawning.

Two different species of ants may live in separate quarters of the same nest. Many small insects are kept as pets. Nearly two thousand different species of insects have been found in ant nests. They have domesticated more different animals than man has.

Not all such tenants, however, are welcome. Tiny crickets love snug quarters that the ants have excavated with so much toil. Savage beetles also invade the nest.

But ants have worse enemies. Many birds eat them. So do lizards and toads. The giant anteater of South America licks them up by hundreds with his sticky tongue. Native tribes are fond of ants. Honey-pot ants are a delicacy among Mexican Indians. Even Europeans have found that fried ants taste like toasted pecans.

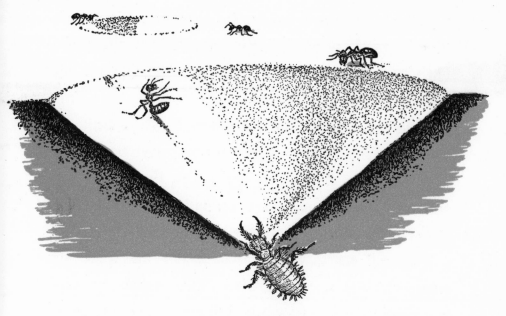

At the bottom, the ant lion is waiting for an ant to fall in.

Strangest of all ant enemies is a curious insect that resembles a dragonfly. It is quite harmless, but in its larval form it is that monster called an ant lion which is less than half an inch long. Its six legs are so weak it can walk with difficulty and then only backward. It has six eyes. It has no mouth but its widespread jaws, armed with sharp spikes, are hollow tubes through which it sucks its food. It digs a cone-shaped hollow in the sand, then buries itself at the bottom with only its jaws showing. An ant comes to the edge of this pit, ventures a little way down, then starts sliding on the loose sand. If it seems likely to escape, the ant lion hurls sand grains to knock it down. Once within reach of those cruel jaws, its body is soon sucked dry. Children in the country call the ant lion a "doodle bug."

Bees are our friends, but ants are rivals and often enemies. True, they do some good. In European countries they are encouraged to build nests about fruit trees where they kill harmful insects.

But they are often a nuisance. They disfigure our lawns. They damage growing crops. In the country they get into our food. And in the tropics they do worse things. In the valley of the Amazon they make life almost unbearable. Some species will gnaw a suit of clothes to rags in a single night. Vegetation swarms with what are known as fire ants. They are so filled with formic acid that brushing against them is like touching a flame. A huge ant nearly an inch long is called the terrible ant. Its bites may cause a fever. And so this fertile valley, nearly as large as the United States, has fewer inhabitants than the Sahara. No wonder it has been called the Kingdom of the Ants!

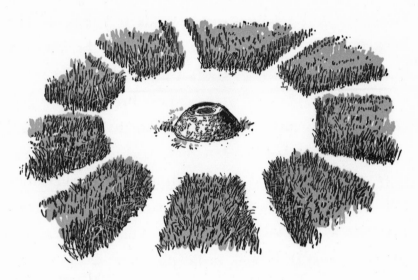

Roads lead out from the ant mound like spokes of a wheel.

Some Interesting Ant Species

Among the swarming billions of ants, some species deserve special mention. Noteworthy are the so-called agricultural ants of Texas.

These ants erect a mound of earth several feet high. Beneath it they dig extensive chambers. All surrounding vegetation is cleared away except their chief food, ant rice, which is allowed to grow near the nest. Roads are also laid out from this center like the spokes of a wheel. Eighteen different kinds of seeds have been found in granaries underground.

The soldiers have enormous heads and jaws. If one were as big as a man, he would have a head like a bushel basket with jaws six feet across. They bite into seeds to prevent their germinating. Because they also crush seeds for the workers to eat, they have been called "living nutcrackers."

If rice in the granary gets damp, the workers dry it in the sun. If the seeds germinate, they are carried outside where they may take root. And this has caused the belief that these ants really plant crops.

In any case there are ants that do have gardens. These are the sauba ants, also called leaf cutters or parasol ants. In a woodland of tropical America you might see a stream of moving leaves. Each green bit cut out of

Each of these ants is carrying a bit cut from a green leaf.

a leaf is being carried by an ant. Stored in underground chambers, these leaf bits are fertilized by the droppings of certain caterpillars. There they develop a kind of fungus or ant mushroom that the ants eat. When a sauba queen starts a new nest, she carries a bit of this fungus with her in a tiny pocket. We raise mushrooms in the dark, but the ants were doing this long before we learned the secret. They cultivate several kinds of fungus in long underground galleries. The scientist Bates measured one that was two hundred and ten feet long.

Sauba ants are sometimes destructive. For in seeking leaves for their gardens, they may strip a tree. They are also brave fighters and will defend their homes against other savage species.

Ants are so fond of honeydew that Darwin called it their favorite food. They lick it from the leaves or bark of plants or trees. But other insects, particularly the aphids or plant lice, gorge on this sweet liquid. And ants make use of them as collectors. For they bring home aphid eggs and, when they hatch, carry the aphids outside and place them on plants which yield honeydew. Toward night they bring them home again just as farmers call cows from pasture to be milked.

When an ant strokes an aphid's back, the aphid will give off the sweet liquid. During twenty-four hours one was observed to yield forty-eight drops. Perhaps she was the prize cow of the ant herd. Ants even dig rooms for their aphids just as farmers build barns. No wonder they are called "dairying" ants!

Some ants are bad neighbors to other ants. They are desperate fighters, biting off the antennae, legs, and even heads of their foes. One nest of these insect robbers sent out forty-six raiding parties in a single month. When they meet foes as savage as themselves, there is war. One time a war between rival ant communities lasted more than six weeks.

Ants also make slaves of weaker ants. They steal their cocoons; and when these hatch, the young workers labor for their masters. Some slave-making ants depend upon their slaves to feed and care for them.

Most dreaded of all are the army or driver ants. True meat eaters, they are often observed in tropical America but seem most destructive in Africa. A raiding column of these ants may be several inches wide and nearly a mile long. The workers carry cocoons of unborn ants. Soldiers march in front while others protect the flanks and form a rear guard. Observers even re-

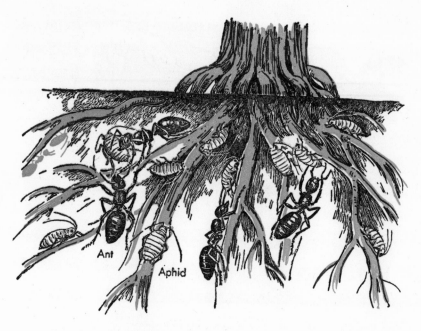

Ants keep aphids for the sweet liquid they give off.

port larger ants that act as officers. Once in motion, the column marches straight ahead. Nothing will stop it except fire or water. Natives flee in terror as army ants march through native huts, destroying all lice, fleas and cockroaches. A British scientist watched a column attack a viper several feet long. Within a few minutes the ants literally tore it to pieces. When the column was disturbed, ants a hundred yards away learned of the interruption within ten seconds. How the news traveled so quickly only the ants could tell us.

Some ants are desperate fighters.

At times army ants gather in circles around a group of larger ants which may be important individuals. At times they collect in a great ball over the roots of a tree where they seem to be asleep. But in motion they have been called the most terrible army in the world. Certainly all other animals give them the right of way.

And so, whether builders or gardeners or dairy farmers or soldiers, ants are truly wonder workers.

Termites Are Master Builders

If you should go for a walk in Africa or Australia, you might come upon a strange mound rising a dozen feet or more. Although made of earth, it would be solid enough to hold your weight. "What a queer heap!" you might say, and you would be right. For you would be facing a city of termites, the master builders of the insect world.

To be sure, bees have cities also, for a single hive may shelter 50,000 of them. Ants build on an even grander scale. An ant colony in Jamaica numbered more than 600,000. But a termite nest in South America was estimated to shelter nearly three million of these strange creatures—a population almost as large as that of Chicago.

Termites are often called white ants. But they are neither ants nor really white. Pale in color, they do look something like ants. But they belong to a different order of insects more nearly related to the cockroaches.

But termites resemble ants in some of their habits. They swarm only once in a lifetime when great clouds of males and females fly away in search of new homes. Almost all of them are eaten by birds or animals or die from other causes. But where a male and female alight together, they begin at once to dig a new home. Shedding their wings, which are now in the way, they mate in their underground apartment, eager to start another termite colony.

Male bees are thrust out of the hive to starve, and

male ants do not live long. But the termite "king" may enjoy a long life with his queen in their royal chamber. One pair were observed to survive for twenty-five years. Meanwhile, the termite queen becomes little better than an egg-laying machine. Her swollen body may be four inches long and look like a fat sausage. She is then more than 150 times larger than her husband although he is bigger than most other termites. During her lifetime, which may last for fifty years, she may lay ten million eggs! Some of these eggs hatch into soldiers. Others from time to time produce males and females, but far the greatest number become workers like the bees. These workers are usually blind. They grope their way through life guided by delicate sense organs upon the antennae, legs and parts of the body. These react to vibrations just as your radio does. In fact, termites seem able to converse by a sort of wireless system all their own.

To build their cities the workers gather grains of earth or sand. With their saliva they stick these together to harden like cement. In this way they erect their mounds which are honeycombed with rooms and galleries like the streets of some great city.

Termite soldiers are larger than the workers, with big

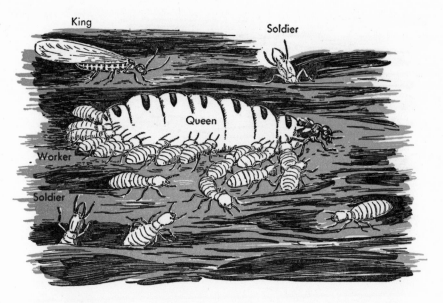

King

Soldier

Queen

Worker

Soldier

The swollen body of a termite queen may be four inches long.

hard heads. When the termite city is attacked, they collect at the entrance. There they pile one on top of the other with only their heads showing. In this way they form a living wall. Other soldiers have long snouts. When attacked by ants, and the two are often at war, the snouted termite discharges a gummy liquid which sticks about the ant soldier's neck like glue. While trying to free his neck, the ant forgets about fighting and is quite helpless.

Termites feed largely upon wood. In Sweden when meat was scarce during wartime, scientists tried to

Termites' taste for wood makes them a destructive pest.

change wood into food. When hamburgers failed, they offered woodburgers which were not very tasty at best. But the termites long ago succeeded where Swedish scientists failed. Their stomachs shelter tiny plants called bacteria which enable them to digest wood. And so they relish a hearty meal of oak or pine or even mahogany.

Their taste for wood makes them a destructive pest. Most of their 2,000 species live in tropical countries. And there a chair may give way beneath you or the very floor sink under your feet. For termites have eaten the heart out of the wood.

In their search for food these curious creatures do

unbelievable things. In Panama where the Smithsonian Institution has been studying their habits, termites have gnawed through lead sheathing about cables. They have even burrowed through five inches of solid cement.

The termite is more common in this country than we might wish. For while he is a wonderful builder, he is also a great destroyer. One species in Florida prefers dry, well-seasoned timber as he gnaws his way into fine homes. Another species in California works upward from the moist earth. Termites cause this country an annual loss estimated at forty million dollars. And that is rather a large bill for so tiny an insect.

Insect Orchestras

On the island of Basilan in the Philippines I once followed a little glade into the jungle and was almost deafened by shrill sounds. For the insects were holding an ear-splitting concert.

If we could gather all the vocal insects together, they would form a remarkable orchestra. Just as male canaries do all the singing, male insects furnish most of the trilling and chirping. They do not really sing, of course.

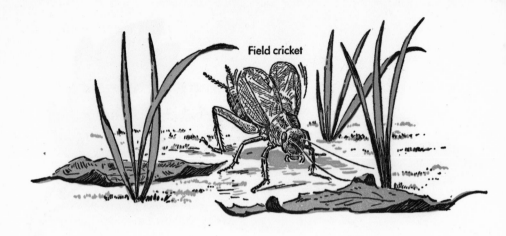

Field cricket

They play. For Nature has provided them with sound makers stranger than any that we use on New Year's Eve.

Perhaps the most accomplished insect musicians are the crickets. Scientists list over two thousand species, but we need to note only a few of them. They are not songsters but fiddlers. On one wing they have a membrane covered with ridges. On the other wing are ridges notched like a file. By rubbing one wing over the other the cricket can make a variety of notes, just as a violinist does when he draws his bow across the strings.

The field cricket strikes a high *treet-treet-treet*, a lower *cree-cree-cree*, and a gruff *gru-gru-gru*. On a still night he can be heard nearly a mile away. The female cricket listens to his serenade with ears that are placed upon her knees.

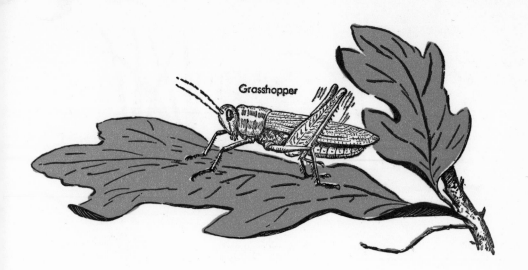

Grasshopper

The snowy tree cricket is the most talented member of the family. One was heard to repeat his note more than two thousand times. Another chirped steadily ninety times a minute. At that rate he would chirp four million times in two months! His wings must be tough, indeed, to stand such punishment.

The house cricket came from Europe but seems contented here. He is a skillful ventriloquist. He does this by shifting his wings and reducing the sound so that it seems to come from different directions.

The mole cricket digs a tunnel with his powerful front paws, then sits at the entrance to his burrow to add his muffled *churp-churp-churp* to the chorus.

Crickets have often been selected like song birds for the sweetness of their notes and kept in tiny cages as pets.

But the leader of the insect orchestra would be the

cicada or seventeen-year locust. Unlike the cricket, he is not so much a fiddler as a drummer. Under his wings are round membranes like drumheads. These are ridged like a washboard and controlled by tiny muscles. The cicada presses these membranes in and out as we might the bottom of a tin pan. And what a racket a swarm of them can make! In the Southern states, schools have even been dismissed because cicadas made so much noise in the trees outside.

Some grasshoppers would add to our insect orchestra. The cone-headed grasshopper makes a loud note by rubbing his wings together. Other species do much the same with their wings against their thighs. And their cousins, the locusts, give off a rustling sound that may be heard a quarter of a mile.

Another musical insect is the katydid which belongs to the grasshopper family but doesn't look it. Here again it is the male who tattles about "katy," but never tells us what she really did. Sometimes he seems to try, for on hot nights he will add a syllable to his brief song. But as the temperature falls, he drops one syllable after another. And his last note stops when the night chill falls below 53 degrees.

For insect musicians are also fairly accurate ther-

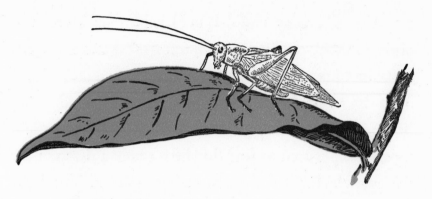

The katydid belongs to the grasshopper family.

mometers. Crickets chirp more rapidly as it grows warmer. But they seldom chirp at all when the temperature rises above 100 or sinks below 55. Some people amuse themselves by estimating heat or cold from cricket songs. Count the number of chirps the snowy cricket makes in 15 seconds then add 40, they tell us, and we have the exact figure. The grasshopper, though less reliable, is more sensitive. For he seldom makes a sound when the temperature drops below 61 degrees.

In every large orchestra minor instruments help out the violins, the horns and the drums. And so it is among the insects. That curious creature, the water boatman, listening in some neighboring pool, adds a squeaky note by rubbing his legs together. So, too, does the larva of a species of sphinx moth. Bumblebees drone like saxophones. Flies, wasps and bees buzz. And even the unwelcome mosquito hums.

In the walls of old houses the larva of the dead-watch beetle makes a sucking, gnawing sound. And at night lonely people used to fear that he foretold a death in the family, which, of course, was quite untrue. The larva was merely digging tunnels in the wood. But most insect songs seem cheerful and happy. And whether they are made as mating calls or from sheer love of sound, they add to Nature's melodies.

Insect Lamplighters

On summer nights the lamplighters are busy in the insect world, sparkling like fairy lanterns. We do not appreciate them as we should although they are one of Nature's wonders. We do not even speak of them correctly for we call them glowworms and fireflies. Yet they are neither worms nor flies but belong to the great order of the Coleoptera or beetles.

Glowworms are fairly numerous in temperate countries. They have been much studied in England where a

Fireflies seem to dance among the shadows.

particular species is interesting for other reasons besides the light it gives. For it shows a far greater difference between male and female than we find in most insects. The male has the horny wings of the true beetle, but the female has no wings at all and looks much like a fat grub or larva.

Both as a larva and a mature insect she attacks snails. The poor snail retires as far as he can crawl into his shell. As the hungry glowworm follows, he pours out slime to protect himself. But she merely thrusts out a fleshy brush from her body with which she wipes off the slime and keeps on eating.

Near her tail she shows a yellowish patch which gives off light. Even her eggs have a faint glow. When they hatch four or five weeks later, both larva and pupa keep on glowing.

The male also glows a little but much less brightly. It is thought the female flashes her light to attract him, for she has no wings. Male glowworms will even fly through an open window toward a lighted lamp. No doubt they think this is an uncommonly large female and are disgusted at their mistake.

Fireflies are most at home in warmer regions, particularly the tropics. There they are a curiosity to persons who see them for the first time. Sir Francis Drake, the second man who ever sailed around the world, first observed them on a little island in the East Indies. He stopped there to repair his ship which had been nearly wrecked upon a rock, and wrote about a "swarm of fiery worms flying through the air."

The female glowworm crawls about in grass and shrubbery. But fireflies seem to dance among the shadows. A number of rather small "fire beetles" are fairly common in this country. But there is a much larger species in the tropics. Rusty brown in color, it carries two oval, yellowish-white spots on its thorax or rather its shoulders and another on the under surface of the abdomen. These give off sparkles which the beetle can turn on or off at will just as we do a battery flashlight. The Indians catch these fireflies by twirling a bit of burning charcoal which attracts them. Kept in little cages, they are purchased by ladies who wear them as ornaments.

The glowworm gives off a greenish glow, the firefly a more brilliant yellow-white flash. And both are among Nature's mysteries. In making light we waste much energy in heat. But these humble insects have learned how to make what scientists call "cold light." This secret they share with strange shrimps and fish in the deep sea where sunlight never comes. Many queer creatures live down there in the darkness. But quite as wonderful are the tiny lamplighters that we miscall glowworms and fireflies.

Insect Enemy Number One—The Mosquito

Insect enemy number one is the mosquito. Many other insects look more dangerous. The mosquito seems frail and weak. A quarter of a million of them would scarcely weigh one pound. But the harm they do is out of all proportion to their size.

To most people a mosquito is just a mosquito. But scientists list some two thousand species. They are found almost everywhere from the equator to the Polar seas.

And everywhere they are a pest both to animals and men. In tropical countries people sleep in beds draped with mosquito netting. In Alaska miners smear their faces with clay as a protection. And great areas of the earth remain almost uninhabited. For there the mosquito has conquered.

Even when mosquitoes do not bite, they disturb our sleep by their humming. They make this sound by vibrating tiny projections across their air passages.

But do not blame the male mosquito. If not a gentleman, he at least does little harm. He feasts on nectar from the flowers or other plant juices. The female mosquito causes all the trouble. She thirsts for blood not alone as food but to enable her to lay her eggs. For most mosquitoes cannot breed without at least one blood meal.

No surgeon's instruments are more skillfully made than hers. Her long proboscis ends in six tiny lancets. Two of these are barbed. Another, the largest, is a hollow tube through which she sucks up blood. Through another, also hollow, she pumps saliva into the wound to increase the flow of blood. But her saliva may also contain the germs of dangerous diseases she has picked up elsewhere.

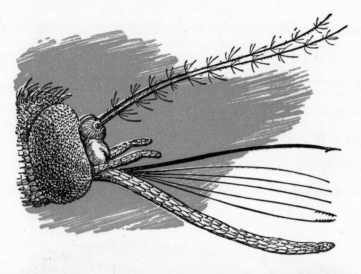

With a microscope we can see the lancets of a mosquito's proboscis. No surgeon's instruments are more skillfully made.

A few species of mosquito are carriers of malaria. It has been estimated that 800 million people suffer from some form of this disease. Tropical types are often deadly. Three million persons have died in a single year. In some countries malaria is the chief problem in the lives of the people. Though more common in hot countries, malaria has been carried to the shores of the Arctic.

Mosquitoes also carry yellow fever, which is less common but more deadly. Early attempts to dig the Panama Canal were abandoned because of malaria and yellow fever. Mosquitoes alone were to blame.

In addition they carry such diseases as dengue or breakbone fever, elephantiasis, and a fatal sleeping sickness that has killed thousands of horses.

The life story of the mosquito is a curious one. At first it is a water baby, for the eggs are always spread upon water and there the larvae develop. A female mosquito lays upward of 400 eggs. These she arranges in a neat raft. Marshes are a favorite breeding place. Puddles

The mosquito which rests with its body tilted may carry disease.

and rain barrels suit her fancy, too. In the tropics she often seeks water that has accumulated in plants or flowers.

Different kinds of mosquitoes grow at different rates. Eggs laid in temporary pools may develop into full-grown mosquitoes in a few days. Those laid in a rain-filled hollow tree may require months.

On hatching, the larvae hang suspended from the surface of the water, breathing through tiny tubes. Then, curling up and bulging, they turn into pupae. Full-grown, the mosquito breaks out of the pupal covering like a chicken from the egg, leaving the empty shell still floating. Her body is now covered with more than twenty thousand fine scales. These and the veins in her wings, which follow a set pattern, enable the scientist to determine her particular species.

The death rate among mosquitoes is terrific. Both eggs and larvae are food for fish and tadpoles and the larvae of other larger insects. Full-grown mosquitoes fall victims to birds and bats and dragonflies. And so mosquitoes seldom live more than a few days. But a few crawl into nooks in trees or walls where they can hibernate through the winter. And some species—the most vicious—can lay eggs without a single drink of blood.

Scientists wage a continuous war against the more dangerous species of mosquitoes. Marshes are drained and stagnant pools are covered with oil so mosquitoes will have no water on which to lay their eggs. Great areas are sprayed from the air to kill the deadly creatures. In many places that were once unhealthy, yellow fever and even malaria have been almost stamped out. But such warfare is costly. Mosquitoes breed by the billion so there are always some that carry on the fight against mankind.

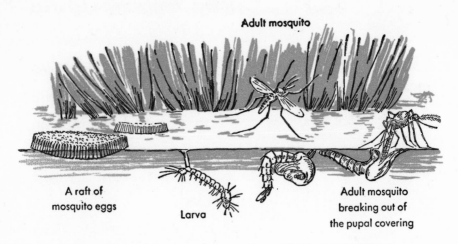

Adult mosquito

A raft of
mosquito eggs

Larva

Adult mosquito
breaking out of
the pupal covering

The eggs of a mosquito are always laid upon water.

But mosquitoes are only the ringleaders in a band of insect killers far worse than any human gangsters. Body lice spread the germs of relapsing fever. They also carry a far worse disease—typhus. This was the dreaded prison fever of the Middle Ages that carried off millions of victims. Though less common now, epidemics of typhus broke out in Italy, Poland, and other countries not many years ago.

Fleas can be even worse offenders, for they carry the germs of bubonic plague. In the Middle Ages this was better known as the Black Death. Fleas carried by rats spread this fearful disease from Asia across Europe. Big cities were nearly abandoned so that grass grew in the streets. The dead were carried out and piled in heaps. Half the people in an entire country sometimes died from the plague. It was dreaded more than famine or invading armies. And it lingers still in Burma, India and central China where it breaks out from time to time.

Insect Wasters and Spoilers

Many of our insect enemies bite and spread disease. There are others that do great damage by wasting or spoiling the things we need in order to live. They devour much of our food. They attack our grain fields and vegetable gardens. They make our finest shrubs and trees wither and die. They ruin our clothes and rugs. They even undermine our very homes.

Ours is a hungry world where half the people seldom get enough to eat, yet insects are always wasting the food supply. Even food upon our pantry shelves is never safe from them. Insects in their larval form are always greedy. Those we call the weevils and the maggots and the worms are among our worst wasters.

It has been estimated that insects destroy more than 300 million bushels of grain in this country every year. This is after all the labor of raising, harvesting and storing it.

But insects are even more destructive to growing crops. Sometimes they sweep the country like invading armies. In the Near East locusts often spread over fields and woodlands eating every green leaf and blade of grass. When they pass on, they leave a desert behind them. And famine often follows.

Grasshoppers sometimes sweep across our Western states spreading ruin everywhere. In 1936 they destroyed more than a hundred million dollars' worth of grain.

Such swarms of insects are like forest fires. They ruin great areas and then pass on. But on a smaller scale farmers everywhere must wage an endless fight to protect their growing crops from destructive insects that are always with us. These are the striped squash bugs and the tomato worms and their many other winged or crawling relatives.

Among insects that attack our grain and feed crops are the Hessian fly and the chinch bug. The corn borer is an unwelcome immigrant from Europe. A tiny insect that clings like scales to the bark nearly destroyed the vineyards of France. Here we have the peach-tree borer and the plum curculio. Orange growers dread red-scale insects. Apple orchards are infested by the coddling

Grasshoppers sometimes destroy whole fields of grain.

moth. And there are many more insect offenders.

Other crops also suffer. The larvae of the sphinx and hawk moths gnaw the leaves of the tobacco plant. In our Southern states the boll weevil has done enormous damage. In each one of five different years he caused a loss to cotton growers of more than half a billion dollars.

Insects also eat our woolen clothing and our rugs. It is estimated that in this country such insects every year destroy half a billion dollars' worth of goods.

Many insects drink the sap or juices of plants and so injure shrubs and trees. Others that bore into bark and wood not only harm the trees but let in the spores of fungi which are even worse. In ten years the spruce bud worm had destroyed more than three-quarters of the spruce and balsam forests of Maine and Minnesota. In Canada it had ruined enough growing timber to supply all the paper mills in that region for three full years. The eastern larch has almost disappeared from New England and eastern Canada. It was killed by the larch sawfly. Each year the western pine beetle destroys half a billion board feet of yellow pine among our finest lumber. The loblolly pine is a valuable tree in our Southern states, but nearly half the annual crop is ruined by insects.

Some insects also attack finished lumber after men have gone to all the trouble of cutting and stacking it. They may prefer lumber that has been well seasoned and even used in building homes. In such wood the sawyer beetle cuts out great holes that make it look something like Swiss cheese. The White House in Washington was recently repaired after insects had begun to eat away the very roof beams. They did not hesitate to invade the home of the President. And the cost to our government was several million dollars.

The damage insects do varies from year to year. Exact

figures are not easy to collect. Yet all authorities agree that the annual bill in this country is enormous. Some estimate it at four billion dollars. And that would be about twenty-five dollars for every man, woman and child!

Swat That Fly!

Swat that fly! He gets into our homes all uninvited, and so we call him the housefly. He is also an unwelcome visitor in restaurants and markets. He does not bite, but how annoying he can be! His sticky feet and hairy legs collect all sorts of filth. Then he walks into our butter dish or falls into our glass of milk. Not only

The microscope helps us see what a fly's head really looks like.

is he a nuisance, but he spreads disease. He is blamed for many cases of typhoid and dysentery and even tuberculosis.

The female lays her eggs, which may number several hundred, in spoiling meat or decaying garbage. They hatch into wormlike maggots, and in a brief time—from ten days to two weeks—they are full-grown. They breed at a rate that makes us fairly dizzy. For it has been esti-mated that if a single pair and all their children could multiply unchecked, they would in one year cover the entire land surface of the earth with flies to a depth of 47 feet! No wonder scientists keep repeating "Swat that fly."

And the housefly has even worse relatives. The stable fly looks much like him and sometimes gets into our houses. But it bites! And how it torments the poor horses and cows! It breeds in straw or decaying vegeta-tion and is a continual problem to the dairy farmer.

And it has even more bloodthirsty relatives. Black flies make life wretched for both men and animals in northern latitudes. Big "green heads" are a pest on sum-mer beaches. And there are larger gadflies. In the tropics one species leaves a stream of blood where he bites. Largest of all is a huge fellow in the Amazon Valley.

His outstretched wings are three inches across. Fortunately, he does not bite, but his larvae bore into living trees and drink the sap. The tiny fruit flies do not bite either. But how they swarm about a dish of ripe fruit!

A pest to bee growers is the robber fly. Long-bodied and with a strong proboscis, he pounces upon many a poor bee flying homeward laden with pollen and nectar. True, he also preys upon harmful insects.

Most detested are the botflies and warble flies. The female, darting through the air like a bullet, drives her needle-like ovipositor through the skin of some animal or man and lays an egg. Soon a hairy grub hatches out and squirms and wriggles. Natives in tropical countries cut out the grub with a knife. But the poor animals can get no such relief. Swellings appear, and the skin is greatly injured. The hides of reindeer in the far North have been found fairly riddled by warble flies.

Even worse enemies are the tsetse flies of Africa. For they spread the dreaded sleeping sickness which has carried off natives by the millions. On the shores of beautiful Lake Victoria in Africa, great areas have been abandoned because of this fly. In the French colonies six million natives died from sleeping sickness within a few years; and Uganda, one of the finest districts in all

Africa, lost two-thirds of its population.

"Swat the fly" should be our slogan in a war against other harmful insects in which the whole world is engaged. At our ports we try to keep out those that might come from other countries. Every plant and bulb and root from countries where such insects thrive is disinfected. And if such insects do break through our defenses, we fight them as we would an invading army. When the Mediterranean fruit fly reached Florida, all infested orange trees were burned and great areas sprayed repeatedly. A small army of men once ranged along the Hudson and Champlain valleys to keep the gypsy moth, which was attacking New England trees, from spreading westward.

Other countries are just as watchful and on their guard. We have grown accustomed to the potato beetle, but Europe wants none of it. In England posters are displayed with pictures of the beetle and warnings to farmers to report any they may find.

But insect quarantines are difficult to enforce. Oceans were once a protection and so were deserts. But modern travel spans such barriers in a few days or even hours. Insects, or their eggs, are often concealed in things purchased in far-off places. Insects are also clever stow-

Airplanes spray insecticides on fields and forests.

aways in ships and hitchhikers on automobiles. And they are learning to steal rides on airplanes. In a single year 7,000 visiting planes were found infested with insects. In this way the tsetse fly has invaded the valley of the Amazon. And doctors dread to think what may happen if the germs of yellow fever that mosquitoes carry ever reach the crowded cities of India.

Meanwhile, new insects appear or older forms develop bad habits. The Mexican bean beetle belongs to a family of meat eaters. But it turned vegetarian and now attacks bean plants. Even the potato beetle was once content with a diet of weeds in Colorado where he seems to have originated. Now he insists upon potatoes. Farmers once raised fine apples with little trouble. Now orchards must be sprayed repeatedly.

Many sprays and powders have been developed to kill harmful insects. A favorite is DDT. It has killed flies and mosquitoes by the billion. But it also kills bees. Besides, such pests as grasshoppers, bean beetles and boll weevils do not seem to mind it. Even houseflies finally become immune. Some scientists claim we are only killing the weaker insects and sparing the stronger ones.

Insect breeding places are now attacked. In cities garbage pails must be covered. Swamps are drained to prevent the breeding of mosquitoes. Even forests are sprayed from airplanes and helicopters. In this country alone 200 million dollars' worth of insecticides are manufactured every year.

And so the war goes on, growing more serious and more costly all the time. Few of us ever stop to think how serious it is. Yet scientists tell us that if the harmful insects that destroy our food, our clothing and our homes and threaten us with disease could multiply unchecked, they would in six short years wipe out all human life upon the earth!

No wonder they urge us to "Swat that fly!"

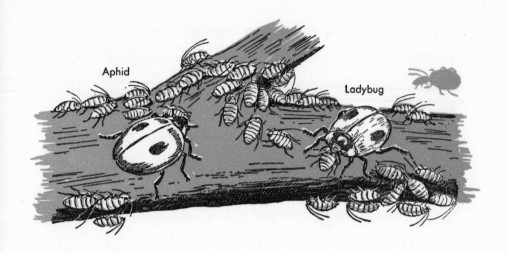

Aphid

Ladybug

Welcome to the Ladybug!

We should all be grateful to a certain chubby, spotted beetle which we call the ladybug. But she is anything but a lady to the aphids that injure our shrubs and trees. When these fuzzy plant lice, often known as mealy bugs, threatened California's orange groves, the ladybug was brought over from Australia because she dotes on mealy bugs. And now men make a business of collecting ladybugs to sell to farmers. Cartons holding 135,000 of them are shipped long distances to help protect the trees and crops.

But ladybugs object to cold weather. And so they

are raised by the million in incubators like chickens. Meanwhile, they demand their usual ration of mealy bugs. While they prefer citrus trees, mealy bugs have been taught to eat potato sprouts. And so potatoes are purchased by the ton to feed to mealy bugs that are fed to ladybugs until the ladybugs are big enough to go out and help the farmers.

But the ladybug is not our only six-legged ally. Insects are their own worst enemies. And every harmful species that threatens us has some mortal enemy in one or more other species.

Thus, the asparagus worm has a deadly foe in a tiny wasp. This wasp is fond of the eggs which hatch such worms and will eat five or six at a time. In this she is like the squirrels and crows which rob birds' nests. But she does something else that no squirrel or crow could do. Into some of the eggs she inserts her own eggs. Both eggs hatch, one within the other. Then the asparagus worm is eaten alive by the tiny grub of the wasp inside its body.

The Japanese beetle has proved to be one of our worst problems. His grubs burrow underground where we cannot get at them. But another small wasp can do this. Digging down, she stings the grub, breaks off a leg or two, drinks some of the body juice and fastens one of her own eggs. The injured grub recovers and begins to eat, but soon the wasp egg hatches. The wasp larva buries its mouth parts in the body of the larger grub and clings until both fat and body juices are consumed.

Among these useful but cruel allies of ours are the ichneumon flies. They, too, belong to the order of the wasps and include over 3,000 species. The female sometimes has an ovipositor several times as long as the rest of her body. Through this she inserts her eggs into the eggs or larvae of other insects where they hatch and do their deadly work.

When harmful insects from other countries break through our defenses, they multiply rapidly because they are not held in check by insect enemies they face at home. And so our government searches all over the world for such insect enemies. It also helps other countries which have been invaded by our own insect pests. Within the past few years hundreds of shipments of such insects, including 138 different species, have been sent abroad.

Our insect allies also help rid us of harmful plants. One of these was known in Europe as the goat weed. When it was found growing on the Pacific Coast in the

Klamath River Valley, it was called the Klamath weed. It crowded out the grass in pasture lands. It poisoned sheep and cattle when they were forced by hunger to eat it. And it spread rapidly from California to Montana. There seemed no way to fight it. And then, in Australia, two beetles were found which fed upon a similar weed. They were about as large as peas, with glossy wings that looked like gun metal. These beetles were brought here, raised by the million like ladybugs, and scattered about in large colonies. Now great areas once overrun by Klamath weed are growing grass once more.

And so, while we swat the fly and crush the mosquito, let us remember that many other insects are helping us. For of all the swarming species that may number millions, scarcely one in twenty does us any harm. They are the bad actors of the family. And even among them only a few are very destructive. In this country six species, which are the worst offenders, cost us two billion dollars every year.

Some scientists even call insects our tiny friends. And that is true of the bees and the dragonflies and the praying mantis and many, many others besides the ladybug and the Klamath beetle.

For in spite of all the leaf-cutters and root-borers and

blossom-spoilers, vegetation still flourishes wherever soil and climate permit. Meanwhile, the insects keep right on multiplying as they have been doing for ages. And each one of them, no doubt, fills its tiny place in the great plan and pattern of life upon this earth.

When Insects Roamed with Dinosaurs

We do not know just when the first insects appeared, but we know they are older than the dinosaurs. For scientists have found their remains in the Carboniferous Age, when those great forests flourished that formed our coal beds. And that was 250 million years ago.

And so, when the first dinosaur waded among the swamps, the air hummed with insect wings and the waters stirred with insect larvae. Dinosaurs ruled the world for a long, long time. But the last one disappeared sixty million years ago. And the insects still lived on.

Dinosaur bones are found in rocks. Their footprints have been preserved in mud that turned to stone. And in Asia Roy Chapman Andrews even discovered dinosaur eggs. But insects are so small and frail! How could we hope that early species left remains that we can see on the earth today?

Yet there are many such remains. Often the softer insect body has disappeared. Only the outlines of the tougher wings may be traced on slabs of slate or shale. But sometimes the body is also traced and even the tiny hairs and scales which covered it.

Florrisant, Colorado, has proved a mine of fossil insects. There volcanoes once surrounded a shallow lake. Insects flying over the water were buried in volcanic dust, which turned to shale. The lake dried up long ago, but many insect bodies were preserved in this shale. From Florrisant alone more than 50,000 insect fossils have been recovered. Similar remains are found in limestone. And at least 150 different localities have yielded specimens.

The most perfect specimens are not in stone but in amber. This is the hardened sap of pine forests which disappeared long ago. The living insect was caught in gummy drops which oozed from the bark. Much amber comes from the shores of the Baltic Sea. This sea covers the area where ancient pine forests once grew, and waves cast up bits of amber along the beach. In such bits over 150,000 insects that lived millions of years ago have been preserved. I often examine amber specimens

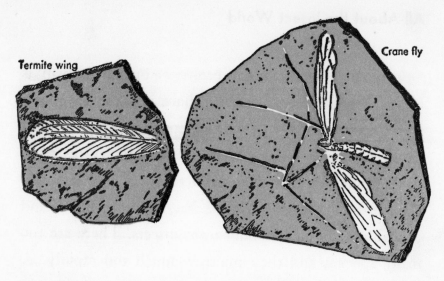

Termite wing

Crane fly

Fossil insects have been preserved in stone and amber.

in my own collection and wonder what the world must have looked like in that far-off time.

Scientists have classified more than 12,000 species of fossil insects. Perhaps the most impressive was the giant dragonfly whose body was fifteen inches long while his wings measured two feet and a half from tip to tip. He may have been the largest insect that ever lived. And as there were no birds then, he ruled the air.

It seems probable that insects were as common in the age of the dinosaurs as they are now. Cockroaches scurried around when the first dinosaur appeared, and they seem to have changed little since that time. Even mosquitoes were abundant forty million years ago. And then, as now, the ants were social creatures.

All About the Insect World

Compared to the other creatures on earth, man is almost a newcomer. Like the dinosaurs, the cave bear and saber-toothed tiger have died out. For as man learned to use his hands and his brain, all other creatures came to fear him. He has conquered even the elephant and the great blue whale. But he has not conquered, and probably never will conquer, the insects. There are too many species, and they multiply much too rapidly. A few harmful ones defy him and even challenge his right to rule the world. And he must fight them in a war that never ends. But all the other insects are either harmless or friendly.

We do not need to go to far-off places in search of adventure. All about us we can find more fascinating scenes and stranger creatures in the great wonderland of the insects.

Index

Index

Index

Mole cricket, 107
Molting, 13
Monarch butterfly, 21–22, *illus.*, 8, 9, 21
Mosquito(es), 4, 7, 12, 42, 110, 113–19 (*illus.*), 127–28, 135
Moth(s), 14, 17, 23–30 (*illus.*). *See also* Silkworm
Mourning cloak butterfly, 19 (*illus.*), 21
Mouth parts, 4
Mud daubers, 84–85, *illus.*, 82
Mule killers, 52
Muscles, 15–16
Musk mare, 61

Nectar, 73–74, 76
Nerve center, 5
Nervous system, 15–16
Noses, 6
Nymphs, 12, 53

Oak gall, 34 (*illus.*)
Ocean, 49
Oxygen, 14

Painted lady butterfly, 19
Paper wasp, *illus.*, 82
Paper-making, 81–82
Peach tree borer, 120
Pearl crescent butterfly, 18 (*illus.*)
Pest(s), 131
Pinch bug, 35
Plant louse. *See* Aphid
Plum curculio, 120
Plumules, 18
Polyphemus (moth), 27
Potato beetle, 64, 126–28
Potato bug, 10
Potter wasp, *illus.*, 82
Praying mantis, 54–58 (*illus.*)
Proboscis, 29, 114, *illus.*, 115

Promethea moth, *illus.*, 23
Propolis, 70
Pupa, 11–12
Purple emperor butterfly, 19–20

Quarantine, 126–27
Queen ants, 87–91, 97
Queen bees, 67, 75–78
Queen termites, 102, *illus.*, 103
Queen wasps, 83

Red admiral butterfly, 18 (*illus.*)
Red scale insects, 120
Regal fritillary butterfly, 19 (*illus.*)
Relapsing fever, 118
Rhinoceros beetle, 35
Rice, 95–96
Robber fly, 125

Saliva, 10, 32
Sauba ants, 96–97
Savage insects, 46, 54
Sawfly, 122
Sawyer beetle, 122
Scarab beetle, 37 (*illus.*)
Segments, 4, 6
Sexton beetle, 38 (*illus.*)
Shell. *See* Body case
Sight. *See* Eye
Silkworm (moth), 30–33 (*illus.*)
Size, 13–16
Skeleton, 6
Sleeping sickness, 116, 125
Slave-making ants, 98
Smell (organ of), 4, 6, 15
Snake doctors, 52
Snowy cricket, 109
Snowy tree cricket, 107
Social insects, 66–67, 81–85
"Social stomach," 91
Soldier ants, 91, 96, 98
Soldier termites, 102–03